PENTECOST 1

INTERPRETING THE LESSONS OF THE CHURCH YEAR

JACK DEAN KINGSBURY

PROCLAMATION 5 SERIES A

FORTRESS PRESS   MINNEAPOLIS

PROCLAMATION 5
Interpreting the Lessons of the Church Year
Series A, Pentecost 1

Cover and interior design: Spangler Design Team

Library of Congress Cataloging-in-Publication Data
(Revised for vol. [5] thru [8])

Proclamation 5.

    Contents: ser. A. [1] Epiphany / Pheme Perkins —
[2] Holy week / Robert H. Smith — [etc.] — [8] Easter /
David Buttrick.
    1. Bible—Homiletical use.   2. Bible—Liturgical
lessons, English.
BS534.5.P765 1993   251   92-22973
    ISBN 0-8006-4177-9 (ser. A, Advent/Christmas)
    ISBN 0-8006-4178-7 (ser. A, Epiphany)
    ISBN 0-8006-4179-5 (ser. A, Lent)
    ISBN 0-8006-4180-9 (ser. A, Holy week)
    ISBN 0-8006-4181-7 (ser. A, Easter)
    ISBN 0-8006-4182-5 (ser. A, Pentecost 1)
    ISBN 0-8006-4183-3 (ser. A, Pentecost 2)
    ISBN 0-8006-4184-1 (ser. A, Pentecost 3)

Manufactured in the U.S.A.   AF 1-4182

97   96   95   94   93   1   2   3   4   5   6   7   8   9   10

CONTENTS

The Day of Pentecost   4

The Holy Trinity
    First Sunday after Pentecost   10

Second Sunday after Pentecost   17

Third Sunday after Pentecost   23

Fourth Sunday after Pentecost   29

Fifth Sunday after Pentecost   35

Sixth Sunday after Pentecost   41

Seventh Sunday after Pentecost   47

Eighth Sunday after Pentecost   53

Ninth Sunday after Pentecost   59

The Day of Pentecost

Lutheran	Roman Catholic	Episcopal	Common Lectionary
Joel 2:28-29	Acts 2:1-11	Acts 2:1-11	Acts 2:1-21 or Isa. 44:1-8
Acts 2:1-21	1 Cor. 12:3b-7, 12-13	1 Cor. 12:4-13	1 Cor. 12:3b-13 or Acts 2:1-21
John 20:19-23	John 20:19-23	John 20:19-23	John 20:19-23 or John 7:37-39

FIRST LESSON: ACTS 2:1-21

In the worship of the early church, the festival of Pentecost supplanted the Jewish festival of the same name. Originally, Israel celebrated Pentecost as the festival of weeks (Exod. 34:22; Deut. 16:10). It occurred fifty days after Passover and marked the conclusion of the grain harvest. Following the destruction of the temple in A.D. 70, however, the Jews used Pentecost to commemorate the covenant that God had made with Israel at Mt. Sinai. In associating the outpouring of the Holy Spirit with the day of Pentecost, Luke apparently gave no thought to the Jewish festival and was simply motivated by his own timetable: Having noted that Jesus' ascension took place forty days after his resurrection (Acts 1:3), Luke chose to identify the outpouring of the Spirit with Pentecost, the "fiftieth day" after the resurrection. For Luke, Pentecost is the "founding day" of the Christian church.

In arranging the worship service, the preacher will not want to lose sight of the meaning Luke ascribes to Pentecost. For Luke, Pentecost is the church's "founding day" because it was then that God empowered apostles and disciples with his Spirit so that they might bear witness to Jesus Christ and the salvation God accomplished in him (2:4, 21). At a time when church membership may not be growing, when church leadership is often thought to be in crisis, and when Christians seem to be less sure than they once were of who they are and what they are about, the temptation for a congregation is to succumb to a siege mentality and to focus ever more intensely on the private spirituality of the individual or group. Pentecost functions as an antidote to this. On Pentecost, Christians are summoned to raise their heads, to look beyond their corner of town, and to recognize anew that God has, in their baptisms, empowered them with his Spirit so that they might assume their place in the long train of all Jesus' disciples and attest to those both near and far that "everyone who calls on the name of the Lord [Jesus] shall be saved" (2:21).

The idea here is not to use worship to sound the false note of triumphalism. Instead, it is to speak of Christian identity and the Christian task, or mission. We Christians are the ones upon whom God has poured out his Spirit (2:17) and we are a diverse lot. We are "sons" and "daughters," "young men" and "old men," and "slaves," both "men and women" (2:17-18). In other words, while we are one in that we all belong to God by virtue of having received the Spirit, we have in no sense been cut from the same cloth: We are women and men, adults and children, rich and poor, privileged and disadvantaged. In his grace, God is no respecter of persons: Claiming all of us as his own, he endows us all with his Spirit.

As a diverse lot empowered with the Spirit, we Christians face a whole world waiting to hear from us, from Parthians, Medes, and Elamites to visitors from Rome, Cretans, and Arabians (2:8-11). To be sure, Luke, in referring to residents of the various nations, envisages exclusively Jews (2:11: "Jews and proselytes"). Regardless, at an early date the church construed Luke's listing of the nations as adumbrating the worldwide mission. In an ancient collect, one hears the church petition God on Pentecost: "Make us messengers of the good news to everyone everywhere." Practically, of course, the way the vast majority of Christians address the world is through support of their denomination's home, world, and social missions or through their own testimony of word and deed to those with whom they interact in their daily lives. However that may be, the thing to note is that Luke, along with the other writers of the New Testament, adjudges that a Christian, to be a Christian, is one engaged in witness. To speak of a Christian as not engaged in witness is a contradiction in terms.

The message the Spirit entrusts to us Christians has to do with the "mighty works of God" (2:11). In Luke's purview, while God's mighty works began with creation and encompass all his saving acts throughout the ages, they reach their culmination in the salvation God has accomplished in Jesus Christ. Here in Acts 2:1-21, the flow of the text is toward the sermon Peter delivers (vv. 14-21). Similarly, the climax of Peter's sermon comes at the end, in his quotation of the word God utters through the prophet Joel to the effect that all those will be saved who call on the name of the Lord Jesus (v. 21). To tell of Jesus as the one in whom God has decisively acted to save is the Christian's joy.

Finally, as we Christians tell of Jesus, we are summoned to do so in the "native language" of those to whom we speak (2:8). In the text, Luke equates speaking in a native language with speaking in a foreign tongue (2:4, 6). In our daily lives, however, the situation is different: To speak in a native language here is more akin to taking a person seriously and addressing him or her with sensitivity, thoughtfulness, and respect. Every person has his or her own native language. One may speak the language of privilege and of worldly wisdom, another the language of alienation, pain, and despair. One may speak the language of receptivity and openness, another the language of anger and defiance. Regardless of the "native language" a person speaks, we Christians draw on the power of the Spirit to address that person in such fashion as that God will lead him or her to call upon the name of Jesus and so be saved.

SECOND LESSON: 1 CORINTHIANS 12:3b-13

At those times when pastors feel beleaguered, they have only to read 1 Corinthians and to ask themselves, "How would you like to have been a pastor in that church?" The whole of Paul's letter is an exercise in problem solving. In the first part (1:10—6:20), Paul addresses problems reported to him by emissaries from Chloe. In the second part (7:1—15:58), he takes up questions the Corinthians have themselves put to him, and the epistle for Pentecost touches on one of these: the request for instruction about spiritual gifts.

The church at Corinth was a gentile congregation (12:2). In the gentile world, ecstatic phenomena of all kinds were held in highest regard. Prophecy, for example, was thought to result when a priest or priestess, indwelt by a god or spirit, began to babble in unintelligible utterances. When interpreted, such utterances counted as oracles. Apparently, the Christians at Corinth were not only familiar with ecstatic phenomena but also avidly practiced them. Looking upon themselves as possessed by the Holy Spirit, they turned their services of worship into individual displays of ecstatic prowess. Rending the air with unintelligible sounds, they spoke in tongues, and it mattered not at all that no one else could understand them (14:9). Among the congregants themselves, these circumstances gave rise to puffery, elitism, and fractiousness.

Paul's strategy for solving this problem was to affirm diversity while emphasizing unity. There are indeed, Paul acknowledges, varieties of "gifts" (12:4), and varieties of "services" and "activities" as well (12:5-6). Without question, he continues, some have the gift of uttering wisdom or knowledge and thus of making known the ways and will of God (12:8). Others have the gift of faith, by which they perform mighty acts, such as miracles (12:9). Still others have the gift of healing (12:9); others, the gift of performing miracles (12:10); others, the gift of prophecy, whereby they edify, encourage, and console fellow Christians (12:10; 14:3); others, the gift of discerning spirits, so as to distinguish the activity of the Holy Spirit from the activity of other spirits or demons (12:10); others, the gift of speaking in tongues (12:10); and others, the gift of interpreting these tongues (12:10). No doubt, each of us Christians, Paul declares, has been given a particular gift.

Still, all these gifts that make us so diverse, Paul insists, are at bottom manifestations of the one Spirit of God (12:7, 11). The one Spirit of God, therefore, is a Spirit of unity. As such, the Spirit empowers each of us to join in the common confession, "Jesus is Lord" (12:3b). Moreover, as we make use of the gift that the Spirit has given us (12:4), the Spirit causes God to be at work in us (12:6) and us to render service to the Lord Jesus (12:5). Through the bond of the Spirit, therefore, we are one in our confession of faith, one with God and the Lord Jesus, and one with one another.

Hence, diverse though we are, Paul concludes, we are nevertheless one. We are, in fact, the body of Christ (12:12): many members of different gender, race, and social status, yet one body (12:13). In baptism, we all received the one Spirit, and the Spirit caused us all to die and rise with Christ and thus to become new creatures incorporated into his body (12:13). United as we are, therefore, we make use of the gift the Spirit has bestowed on us, not to puff ourselves up and to tear down the body of Christ, but to build this body up and to serve the common good (12:7). Consequently, in joy and celebration we all sing and pray on this day of Pentecost, "O come, great Spirit, come!"

GOSPEL: JOHN 20:19-23

In this pericope, John narrates his version of Pentecost and the outpouring of the Holy Spirit. Whereas Luke posits a fifty-day interval between Easter and Pentecost, John knows of no such interval and relegates Jesus' bestowal of the Holy Spirit to Easter Eve (20:19). On the essential point, however, John and Luke agree: The risen and ascending Jesus imparts to the disciples he leaves behind the gift of the Holy Spirit.

In a way that is often typical of texts in John's Gospel, this pericope functions on two levels. At one level, it is part of the narrative John relates and is one of three episodes having to do with appearances of the risen Jesus (20:11-18, 19-23, 24-29). In all three episodes, Jesus reveals himself to followers—to Mary Magdalene, to the eleven, and to Thomas—and leads them to recognize that he, whom they had known and whom they now thought to be dead, has been raised and ascends to the Father. The exultant refrain of "seeing the Lord" is the theme that binds these three episodes together (20:18, 20, 25).

As part of John's narrative, 20:19-23 looks in on the disciples as they are huddled in fear behind locked doors (v. 19). Suddenly, Jesus stands in their midst and dispels their fear with the greeting, "Peace be with you" (v. 19). The peace Jesus grants the disciples is the gift of his presence, which he had earlier promised them (14:27-28). To convince the disciples that he is none other than the one they had previously known, Jesus shows them his hands and his side (v. 20). Recognizing Jesus, the disciples rejoice (v. 20). Uttering the greeting of peace a second time, Jesus commissions the disciples to a ministry in the world that is an extension of his ministry: As the Father sent him into the world, so he sends them (v. 21; 17:18). To empower the disciples for ministry, Jesus, who until now has been the sole bearer of the Spirit in John's story (1:32-33), confers the Spirit on them (v. 22). The task Jesus entrusts to the disciples is one with the task God entrusted him: Through encounter with the disciples, the world is summoned to decide whether or not to accept the forgiveness, light, and life that God proffers in Jesus, his Son (v. 23; 3:16-21).

At a second, figurative level, the church of every age, including both John's church and our own church, can find itself etched in this pericope. It is as though John minted this pericope with an eye to the worship of the church. The picture of the risen Jesus standing in the midst of the assembled disciples conjures up the image of the local church gathered for worship. An air of expectancy fills the sanctuary, for great things are about to happen. The drama of worship begins as the church, in the name of the triune God, invokes the presence of God and therefore the presence of the risen Jesus. As the service of word and sacrament unfolds, the risen Jesus conveys to the church his greeting of peace and grants it the gift of himself. In the Sacrament of the Supper, Jesus shows the church his hands and his side; he gives the church to "see" him as the crucified and risen Lord, and to rejoice in the salvation God has accomplished in him. And through word and sacrament, Jesus commissions the church anew to its ministry to the world.

As with the first disciples, the church's ministry is an extension of Jesus' own ministry. As God sent Jesus into the world, so Jesus sends the church into the world (17:18). To equip the church for its ministry, Jesus bestows on it the Holy Spirit, as in the Sacrament of Baptism. Indeed, through bestowal of the Spirit Jesus creates and enlivens the church as the end-time people of God, just as God, at the beginning, created the first human being and enlivened him with the breath of life (Gen. 2:7). In its ministry to the world, the church forgives and retains sins (20:23). As Matthew envisages this, the church proclaims the gospel of the kingdom throughout the world and summons all nations to become disciples of Jesus (Matt. 24:14; 28:18-20). As Luke envisages this, the church proclaims Jesus to the nations and calls them to repentance and proffers them the forgiveness of sins (Luke 24:47; Acts 4:12). As John envisages this, the church, like Jesus, stands as "light" in the world (3:17-21). Those who come to the light will be saved. Those who do not come to the light thereby show that they love darkness and are evil; their lot will be condemnation. However one assesses these different views, at bottom all three evangelists are concerned to stress one major truth: that it is through encounter with the church that the world decides for or against Jesus and therefore for or against the salvation that God proffers the world in him. In worship, the risen Jesus touches the church with God's grace, enlivens it with the Spirit, and sends it forth to minister to the world.

The Holy Trinity
First Sunday after Pentecost

Lutheran	Roman Catholic	Episcopal	Common Lectionary
Gen. 1:1—2:3	Exod. 34:4b-6, 8-9	Gen. 1:1—2:3	Deut. 4:32-40
2 Cor. 13:11-14	2 Cor. 13:11-13	2 Cor. 13:11-14	2 Cor. 13:5-14
Matt. 28:16-20	John 3:16-18	Matt. 28:16-20	Matt. 28:16-20

FIRST LESSON: GENESIS 1:1—2:3

Initially, the festivals Christians observed commemorated events in the life of either Jesus or the church: Easter, the earliest festival, commemorated the resurrection; Pentecost, the second festival, commemorated the outpouring of the Spirit on the disciples; and Epiphany, the third festival, commemorated the incarnation, God's manifestation of himself in the birth and baptism of Jesus. Not until later centuries did the church institute festivals such as that of the Holy Trinity, which is held in honor of a church doctrine. Originating in Europe, Holy Trinity was especially popular in England, France, Germany, and the Netherlands. As a result, it became tradition among Lutherans and Anglicans to number the Sundays of the second half of the church year not after Pentecost but after Trinity.

Genesis 1:1—2:3 contains the so-called Priestly account of creation, which achieved its final form at the time of Israel's exile. Although the focus of the account is on God, the creator, Christians have customarily found in it allusions to the Son and the Spirit: to the Son, because God creates by the word of his mouth (see John 1:1-3); and to the Spirit, because the account tells of a wind from God (the Spirit of God) moving over the face of the waters (1:2). These alleged trinitarian allusions explain why Gen. 1:1—2:3 has found its way into the lectionary as the Old Testament lesson for Holy Trinity.

Fierce quarrels between creationists and evolutionists have caused many Christians to misjudge the nature of Gen. 1:1—2:3. As one commentator puts it, this account contains Priestly doctrine—declarations of faith—concerning the world and human life as they exist under the lordship of the God who redeemed Israel and chose it to be his people. The knowledge contained in this account, therefore, is faith-knowledge, not scientific knowledge. Whereas faith-knowledge dares to speak about God and how he relates to the world, scientific knowledge, because it is derived from the application of a method that relies on physical observation and experimentation, must prescind from this. Faith-knowledge addresses dimensions of reality that are inaccessible to the tools and hypotheses of science.

As the sermon text for Holy Trinity, Genesis 1 invites the preacher to explore the vision of God it projects. In Genesis 1 God, the creator, is first of all the "Lord" of creation. Although to say this may seem commonplace, the fact of the matter is that this truth tends to get lost in most popular notions of God.

The reason is that such popular notions often identify God merely with some aspect of creation. For many people, God is to be understood as in some sense "up there" in the stars; the telltale sign of this belief is the assiduous reading of horoscopes. For others, God is to be found "out there" in nature; those who think this see it as their religious task to align their lives with nature's rhythms. For still others, the place of God's existence is "deep down inside" his creatures; those who believe this strive to get in touch with God by probing the recesses of their inner selves.

For Genesis 1, however, to confess God as creator is to affirm equally that he is distinct from creation and that creation belongs to him (v. 1). Already before creation, God existed, and God created all things as a free act of his will. It is in this sense that Genesis 1 attests to God as the Lord of creation. So where does God give himself to be known? The answer to this question comes not from Genesis but from the New Testament: in Jesus Christ.

God, the Lord of creation, is supremely a God of order. For the vast majority of people today, this article of faith runs counter to present human experiences of nature and history. World order seems to be teetering on a precipice. Nature is wreaking her vengeance on humankind for burning her forests, poisoning her waters, and polluting her air. War and terrorism put the lie to every new age of peace that is proclaimed. In the face of signs that history and nature are spinning out of control, Genesis 1 boldly asserts that God, the creator, tames chaos and governs the world (vv. 1-2). The earth, says Genesis 1, is like a disk surrounded by the waters of chaos: the primeval waters below, the heavenly waters above, and the oceans on all sides (vv. 6-9). The only reason earth survives the forces of chaos is that God uses his creative power to ensure its survival. Just as God ensures the order of the world, however, so he also governs the course of the world. Humankind flouts the order God has established in creation and his governance of history only at its peril. Still, because God is in control of creation and history, we children of God can rest assured that our hope for a better world and a better future—for a new world and a new future—is not in vain.

As a corollary to the truth that God is a God of order, Genesis 1 stoutly affirms that God makes all things "good" (vv. 4, 10, 12, 18, 21, 25, 31). It belongs to our condition that we humans worry incessantly about God's disposition toward us and our world. Theologically, this is the age-old question of theodicy: Is it not indisputable that the existence of evil disproves the notion that God is good? Genesis 1 deals with this question only indirectly. Regardless, it powerfully urges the believer to infer the goodness of God from the goodness of the creation he brought into being. God, Genesis 1 avows, made all things good, which is to say that God is not the one who injected the virus of sin and evil into his creation. In point of fact, to learn of this one must turn to Genesis 3. No, God demonstrated in making all things good that he is well disposed toward the world and humankind, and in saving the world in Jesus Christ, he has revealed that his intentions toward the creation are ultimately gracious.

SECOND LESSON: 2 CORINTHIANS 13:5-13

If one wonders why this text has been chosen to be read on Holy Trinity, one need look no farther than the blessing one finds in 13:13. Otherwise, 13:5-13 constitutes the conclusion of the vigorous letter Paul wrote to the Corinthians in defense of his apostleship (chaps. 10–13).

What exactly lies behind Paul's words in 13:10? Why has he written the Corinthians, that, when coming to them, he will not have to use the authority Christ has given him to deal harshly with them? Some years before, Paul had founded the Corinthian congregation, and soon he would visit it for a third time (12:14; 13:1). Recently, however, reports had reached him to the effect that "outsiders" had wormed their way into the congregation and were threatening to take control of it

(11:4). No lightweights, these outsiders promoted themselves with extravagant letters of recommendation (10:12; 3:1). Skilled in oratory (11:6), they proclaimed "another gospel" from that of Paul (11:4). Proud of their Jewish heritage (11:22) and eager to authenticate their status as rival apostles (11:12-13), they boasted of ecstatic experiences (12:1) and performed great signs, or miracles (12:12).

They also attacked Paul. Paul, they said, is a spiritual weakling (10:1): As an orator, he is contemptible; and though he writes strong letters while away, in person he is devoid of spiritual power (10:10). Not only that, but he is also a con man, professing to preach the gospel but in reality concerned to enrich himself (11:7-9). Paul, so the charge went, was a bogus apostle who practiced a bogus ministry.

With these outsiders sowing deep dissension in the Corinthian congregation (12:20-21), Paul writes the letter associated with 2 Corinthians 10–13 to set the record straight about the nature and purpose of his apostleship. Paul's intention is to rectify the situation in Corinth before his visit, so that when he arrives, he can come in peace and not as a harsh disciplinarian (13:10). Accordingly, following his defense of his apostleship and with an eye to his impending visit, Paul closes his letter by issuing a double challenge to the Corinthians: They are to put not him but themselves to the test (13:5), and they are to do not what is evil but what is right (13:7).

In 13:5-6, then, Paul challenges the Corinthians to test themselves. Specifically, they are to determine whether they are in fact "living in the faith," that is, living in conformity with the gospel he preached and they received (v. 5). If the Corinthians pass their test, they will realize both that Christ dwells in them as the one who grants life and summons to obedience (v. 5) and that he, Paul, was not the failure in ministering to them that his opponents make him out to be (v. 6).

In 13:7-9, Paul exhorts the Corinthians to do not what is evil but what is right. For the Corinthians to do what is right is for them to do the will of God, to be wholehearted in their obedience to Christ (v. 7; 10:6). If the Corinthians are obedient to Christ, then it matters little, finally, whether they judge him to be an apostle of whom they can approve or a failure (v. 7). Regardless of how the Corinthians judge him, Paul insists that he, through his ministry, serves the truth of the gospel (v. 8). Indeed, should the Corinthians actually be strong in faith yet perceive him to be weak, then he will rejoice, for it is in weakness that power is truly to be found (v. 9; 12:9).

In preparing a sermon on 13:5-13, the preacher may find it helpful to observe that in this text, as in the whole of 2 Corinthians 10–13, the clash is between a "theology of glory" and a "theology of the cross." The rival apostles represent a theology of glory. They have no truck with the cross of Christ and regard themselves as already reigning with the risen Christ. Their game, therefore, is one of power: They adjudge themselves to be above others, and they are bent not on serving, but on being served; indeed, they perhaps see no need even to submit to the moral constraints of the Christian life (12:21). In contrast, Paul represents a theology of the cross. For him, the true apostle or the true Christian is one whose life is shaped by Christ's cross. To be shaped by Christ's cross is to serve Christ and others, not self; and one way to serve Christ and others is to submit to the moral constraints of the Christian life. Consequently, in challenging the Corinthians to test themselves and not to do evil, Paul enjoins them to live in obedience to the Christ who died for them and lives in them.

GOSPEL: MATTHEW 28:16-20

Matthew's gospel-story is one of conflict. At the human level, Jesus enters into conflict not only with Israel but also with the disciples. Here in 28:16-20, Matthew first tells of the resolution of Jesus' conflict with the disciples (vv. 16-17) and then depicts Jesus as commissioning the disciples to their worldwide mission (vv. 18-20). The reference to Father, Son, and Holy Spirit in the Great Commission strikes the exalted theme of Holy Trinity Sunday.

In 28:16-17, Matthew tells of the resolution of Jesus' conflict with the disciples. At the heart of this conflict is the disciples' persistent refusal to accept Jesus' word that servanthood is the essence of discipleship (16:24). Because the disciples refuse to accept Jesus' word, they are unable to persevere with him during his passion: Judas betrays him (26:49), all the disciples forsake him and flee (26:56), and Peter denies him (26:75). Subsequent to his betrayal of Jesus, Judas goes out and hangs himself (27:5). Hence, Matthew's remark that "eleven" disciples go to Galilee is in keeping with these earlier events.

The reason the eleven go to Galilee is that the two Marys (Mary Magdalene and Mary, the mother of James and of Joseph; 27:56) inform them of the risen Jesus' command to do so (28:10). At the time the two Marys receive Jesus' command, the eleven are still the scattered sheep who are fleeing from Jesus (26:31). In referring to the eleven as "my brothers" (28:10), Jesus shows that even though they have aban-doned him, he has not abandoned them. When, therefore, the two Marys convey Jesus' command to the eleven and the latter do find their way to Jesus in Galilee (28:16), the reader knows that it is by the power of his word that Jesus has "gathered" the scattered disciples. "Gathering the scattered" is a metaphor for reconciliation. Accordingly, on the mountain in Galilee Jesus reconciles the disciples to himself and brings the conflict between him and them to a happy resolution.

As a setting, the "mountain" has special significance (28:16). It is the place where heaven touches earth. Reaching to heaven, the top of the mountain connotes nearness to God. It is, therefore, a place of revelation.

Atop the mountain, the risen Jesus reveals himself to the eleven disciples. Suddenly, he appears before their eyes (28:17), and they see him as the risen one who still bears on his person the marks of the crucifixion (28:5-6). Seeing Jesus as the crucified yet risen one, the disciples at last comprehend the very thing they have thus far refused to comprehend, to wit: that service even unto death lay at the heart of Jesus' ministry (16:21) and that, in like manner, servanthood lies at the heart of discipleship (16:24).

If, however, we are to imagine that Jesus does lead the eleven to new insight, how is one to explain Matthew's remark that they "worshiped him, but some doubted" (28:17). Does not the disciples' "doubt" put the lie to the notion that they "comprehend"? Matthew indicates in chapter 14 how he construes doubt. As Jesus rescues Peter from drowning, he chides him, "O little-faithed one, why did you doubt?" (14:31). On Matthew's view, doubt, while it does indeed connote "little faith," does not connote "no faith." Because disciples of little faith are nevertheless disciples who believe, such disciples still "see and understand." In fact, Matthew suggests that the membership rolls of the church will, to the end of time, contain the names of disciples of both great faith and little faith. While Matthew does not laud disciples of little faith, neither does he exclude them from participating in the work of the church. Jesus enjoins them, too, to engage in ministry.

Having revealed himself to the eleven disciples, the risen Jesus next delivers the Great Commission, entrusting the disciples with the task they are to undertake to the close of the age (28:18-20). As a preface to this commission, Jesus claims authorization to deliver it by virtue of the fact that God has, through exaltation, endowed him with universal authority in heaven and on earth (v. 18). In other words, the task with which the risen Jesus entrusts the church is unlike that of any other organization or group because the Lord of the universe has determined it.

The commission itself is not primarily to "go" but to "make disciples" of all nations (v. 19). At a time when the church is shrinking in numbers and is virtually ignored in the world's councils of power, it is ludicrous for preachers to look backwards in time and to use a sermon based on the Great Commission as an opportunity to flail the church for allegedly harboring imperialistic or triumphalistic intentions. The problem today is that the church is in grave danger of turning in on itself and settling for an understanding of mission that is parochial and less than global in scope. In obedience to the exalted Christ and keenly aware of its own frailty, the church dares to proclaim to the whole world the salvation that God has accomplished in Jesus Christ.

The eleven are to make disciples of all nations by baptizing and teaching (28:19-20). Baptism is carried out in the name of the triune God: Father, Son, and Holy Spirit. Still, Matthew's theology is not yet that of the church of Nicea and Chalcedon. For Matthew, the Father is God, whose Son is Jesus and whose child is the disciple, and whom the disciple loves with heart, soul, and mind (22:37-38). The Son, of course, is Jesus, who reveals the Father to the disciple (11:27) and who, in his death, accomplishes salvation (26:28); the Son is the one whom the disciple is to emulate by internalizing his teaching. And the Spirit is the divine power that enables the disciple to lead the life of discipleship.

As a word of the crucified yet risen Jesus, the Great Commission holds up to the eleven disciples a grand vision buttressed by a solemn pledge. The grand vision is that of the disciples, or church, engaged in the worldwide task of making disciples of all nations. The solemn pledge is that he, the risen Jesus, will enable them to discharge their mission by granting them the sustaining power of his abiding presence (28:20).

Second Sunday after Pentecost

Lutheran	Roman Catholic	Episcopal	Common Lectionary
Deut. 11:18-21, 26-28	Deut. 11:18, 26-28, 32	Deut 11:18-21, 26-28	Gen. 12:1-9
Rom. 3:21-25a, 27-28	Rom. 3:21-25a, 28	Rom. 3:21-25a, 28	Rom. 3:21-28
Matt. 7:21-29	Matt. 7:21-27	Matt. 7:21-27	Matt. 7:21-29

FIRST LESSON: DEUTERONOMY 11:18-21, 26-28

Deuteronomy depicts Moses as delivering a series of addresses to Israel as it is about to enter the promised land of Canaan. Our text is embedded in Moses' second address (4:44—28:68), in a section in which he exhorts Israel to covenant faith (5:1—11:32). In this exhortation, Moses stresses that God chose Israel to be his people, not because Israel can lay any claim to righteousness, but solely by reason of his love and the oath which he swore to the fathers (7:7-8; 9:6). Still, to be elected by grace is not to be exempted from obligation. This is the note that Moses strikes in 11:18-21, 26-28.

In 11:18-21, Moses enjoins Israel, as God's elect, to be ever mindful of God's commandments and to inculcate them in its children with a view to serving God by obeying them. In 11:26-28, Moses promises Israel that it will be blessed if it is obedient to God's commandments and cursed if it is not.

The impact that Moses' injunction to be ever mindful of God's commandments had on later Jews is hard to overestimate. So seriously, in fact, did Jews take it that they turned the words "you shall bind them as a sign on your hand, and fix them as an emblem on your forehead" (11:18) into the custom of wearing phylacteries. Phylacteries are small leather boxes that a Jewish male above thirteen years of age tied to his forehead and left arm at the time of morning prayer. The phylactery tied to the head was divided into four compartments, each of which contained one of the passages of Scripture thought to authorize the use of phylacteries: Exod. 13:1-10, 11-16; Deut. 6:4-9; 11:13-21. The phylactery tied to the left arm had but one compartment, and this contained a parchment on which all four of the scriptural passages were written. To honor the injunction of 11:20—to write God's words on the "doorposts of your house and on your gates"—later Jews also developed the custom of affixing small receptacles containing Deut. 6:4-9 and 11:13-21 to the upper part of the right hand doorpost of their homes. Still today, these two customs are firmly embedded in Jewish ritual.

How did the first hearers of 11:18-21, 26-28 appropriate these words? Within the context of Deuteronomy, Moses addresses them to the generation of Israel that is about to enter the promised land. Most likely, however, the generation that first heard them was the one that went into exile following the destruction of Jerusalem (587 B.C.). For this generation, "blessing" and "curse" were not simply theoretical alternatives. On the contrary, they had taken on historical form. Because of its disobedience to God's law, this generation already knew itself to have come under God's curse. The land and cities of Judah, and especially Jerusalem, had suffered devastation and ruin, and the people had been carried off to Babylon as slaves. The hope that vv. 18-21, 26-28 held out to this generation was that if it repented and turned to God, God's blessing would follow. The constant in all this, however, was that Israel must obey God's commandments. The generation that first heard vv. 18-21, 26-28 appropriated these words by recalling Israel's past as described by Deuteronomy so as to assess the present and discern the future.

The church, too, best appropriates 11:18-21, 26-28 by recalling its past so as to assess the present and discern the future. The church's past, however, is not simply identical with that of Israel. For Deuteronomy, God's great act of salvation was that he chose Israel, redeemed it from bondage in Egypt, and promised it a land. For the church, God's great act of salvation is to be identified with the cross and resurrection of Christ. In Christ's cross and resurrection, God effects the salvation of all and, in light of the Christ event, summons all to obedience, to the doing of his will. Salvation in Christ, therefore, does not exclude blessing and curse.

So, then, in remembrance of God's saving act in Christ and its own subsequent history of doing the will of God—of choosing between blessing and curse—the church assesses the present and faces the future. Today, the church is being pressed as perhaps never before in its history to rethink both what it is and what it is about. No aspect of the church's faith and life is exempt from the pull and tug of scrutiny and debate.

How shall the church understand the nature and purpose of ministry, ordained and lay, in today's world? How shall the church speak of the triune God it worships and serves? Are Father, Son, and Holy Spirit inviolate? Or are they primarily the product of a patriarchal culture? How can the church legitimately make its Scriptures and liturgical language more inclusive? How is one to preach the gospel so that preaching today carries with it the same sense of urgency as in other generations? How can the church better sensitize itself so as to rid itself of all forms of sexism and racism? How shall the church engage in evangelism in a pluralistic society and world? How can the church best respond to the vast social needs confronting people today? As it addresses these questions, Deuteronomy summons the church to remember its past so that the past can shed light on the present and inform the church's vision of the future.

SECOND LESSON: ROMANS 3:21-28

Theologically, Rom. 3:21-28 is thought by many to be the richest passage in the whole of Paul's Epistle to the Romans. It is a powerful exposition of Paul's gospel of justification by grace through faith.

To grasp Paul's statements in 3:21-28, it is important to understand his view of sin. For Paul, sin is not something one jokes about or trifles with; it is a pernicious power that enslaves humans and alienates them from God (3:9-11). In taking such an utterly serious view of sin, Paul places himself at odds with the notion of sin that largely pervades Western society. In American culture, for example, sin—if one admits to its existence at all—is popularly regarded as ignorance, or a lack of adequate knowledge. Conversely, the antidote to sin (i.e., salvation) is often thought to reside in effective education. To recognize this, one has only to consider how we as a society attempt to deal with moral problems that beset us. Is the problem one of teenage pregnancies? Sex education is the answer. Is the problem one of personal or corporate ethics? Devise classes and seminars that teach moral behavior. Is the problem one of cigarette smoking or of alcohol or drug abuse? Educate the public against the use of cigarettes or the abuse of alcohol or drugs. Is the problem one of poor race relations? Have the schools instruct students in good race relations. And so it goes, on and on, with deadly serious matters such as AIDS and with minor matters such as voluntarism.

Now make no mistake, the quarrel here is not with education but with the idea that sin, or evil, is not so radical a problem that it cannot be overcome by the impartation of knowledge about what is good. In contrast, Paul understands sin as a corrupting power that governs us humans in our innermost selves. Born into the world, we embrace sin and sin takes us captive. Though this need not be inevitable, the fact of the matter is that it always happens, in the case of each of us. The upshot is that we all are "without excuse" and stand condemned before God (3:22-23).

Against the backdrop of this woeful verdict, Paul now turns to a clarion proclamation of the gospel. He begins by asserting that God has disclosed his righteousness apart from the law (3:21). The key expression "the righteousness of God" refers to God as rescuing us humans from our enslavement to sin by restoring us to a right relationship with himself. Such a relationship cannot be restored by obedience to the law, for the function of the law is to convict of sin (3:20). No, the possibility of living in a right relationship with God—whereby we acknowledge God to be God and obey him as creatures ought to obey their creator—is given us by God himself as an unmerited gift.

The reason God restores us to a right relationship with him has nothing to do with anything in us but singularly with the death of Christ. Through Christ's shedding of his blood, God expiated, or blotted out, our sin, thus "releasing" us from sin's power (3:25). Such releasing Paul calls "redemption" (3:24), a term the ancients used to refer to the release of slaves from their servitude through the payment of a price. The price God paid was the death of his Son. Having released us from the power of sin, God places us under his power, or lordship. Living in the sphere of God's lordship, we are free to acknowledge him as God and to obey him. Thus, God "justifies" us and puts us in a right relationship with him (3:24, 26).

Still, because God effects our redemption (release from the power of sin) and justification (being in a right relationship with him) only through the death of Christ, such redemption and justification can become personal realities for us solely through "faith" in Christ (3:22, 25-26, 28). To have faith in Christ means, variously, to trust that by virtue of Christ's death God has in fact restored our broken relationship with him; to admit freely that we ourselves are unable to restore this relationship; and to accept humbly the gracious action on our behalf that God undertook in Christ's cross.

One more comment. In 3:25-26, Paul again speaks of God's righteousness. This time, however, the righteousness of God does not connote God's power to deliver from sin but his faithfulness. In Paul's view, God is faithful to us, his faithless creatures, precisely by not surrendering us to the clutches of sin and the fateful consequences of our ungodliness. This having been noted, the organ can now begin to swell as we raise our voices in praise of God.

GOSPEL: MATTHEW 7:21-29

Not for nothing is Matthew's Gospel called the apocalyptic Gospel. In 7:21-29, Matthew juxtaposes a scene depicting the last judgment (vv. 21-23) to the parable of the house built on a rock (vv. 24-27) so as to summon the Christians of his church to do the will of God.

In 7:21-23, Matthew's Jesus looks to the future and imaginatively sketches a scene describing the last judgment. At center stage in this scene are unidentified followers who stand before him as judge and appeal to him as "Lord" (v. 22).

Is it possible to identify these followers more precisely? In this scene, they refer to themselves as prophesying, casting out demons, and performing miracles (v. 22). Acts such as these are typical of prophets. Significantly, Matthew portrays Jesus in the preceding pericope as warning the disciples to "beware of false prophets, who come to you in sheep's clothing but inwardly are ravenous wolves" (7:15). Apparently, Matthew has these same false prophets in view here in vv. 21-23. These prophets have found a place in Matthew's community. The members of the community do not see in them dangerous wolves whose deeds are evil but sheep whose deeds are good (7:16-19). In short, these prophets give the appearance of being as "Christian" as the rest of the community.

Regardless of appearances, however, Jesus says that he will charge these prophets at the latter day with not doing the will of the heavenly Father and with being workers of lawlessness (vv. 21, 23). What is it about the deeds of these prophets that could possibly earn for them such a severe indictment? After all, is it not the case that they act "in Jesus' name"?

In Matthew's view, followers of Jesus do the will of God when they come after Jesus and internalize his teaching. At the core of Jesus' teaching is the summons to love God with heart, soul, and mind and the neighbor as self (22:37-40). Fundamentally, therefore, what Jesus teaches his followers is to serve God and neighbor.

With this in mind, consider again these false prophets. On what basis do they plead their case before Jesus, the judge? On the basis of their having served God and neighbor? Not at all! They rather plead their case by pointing to the marvelous works they have done: They have prophesied, exorcised demons, and performed miracles. In other words, at the root of Matthew's antipathy toward these prophets is his contention that they have made themselves guilty of lawlessness because they do their marvelous deeds not to serve God or neighbor but themselves. All along, Matthew insists, they have been concerned to do not God's will, but their own will.

Lest we be too quick to condemn these false prophets, we would do well to remind ourselves that the line that separates the doing of God's will from the doing of our own will is fine indeed. Most Christians want nothing more than to follow Jesus and to do God's will. To be sure, Hollywood and television regularly portray "good Christians" as hypocritical, intolerant, humorless, and bigoted. But this is caricature. The truth of the matter is that Christians tend to be sincere in their worship, generous in giving of their time and money, open toward others, and concerned about the public good. This notwithstanding, the false prophets serve as an object lesson exactly because they do cross over the fine line. Ironically, they appear not even to have noticed this. Observe the surprise they express in the questions they ask (7:22). The false prophets, imagining that they are doing God's will, in reality pursue their own glory. Human motives are always mixed, never pure. It is easy for us to deceive ourselves. In the name of serving God, we promote ourselves. Under the guise of altruism, we seek our own advantage. In professing to do the will of God, we fix our eyes on our own objectives. This is why the parable of the house built on a rock is important (7:24-27). It summons us to be wise and not foolish (vv. 24, 26). Ultimately, we will stand or fall before Jesus, our judge, depending upon whether we are guided in life by him or by our own lights. Test yourselves, the parable says. The line is fine. Don't be deceived.

Third Sunday after Pentecost

Lutheran	Roman Catholic	Episcopal	Common Lectionary
Hos. 5:15—6:6	Hos. 6:3-6	Hos. 5:15—6:6	Gen. 22:1-18
Rom. 4:18-25	Rom. 4:18-25	Rom. 4:13-18	Rom. 4:13-18
Matt. 9:9-13	Matt. 9:9-13	Matt. 9:9-13	Matt. 9:9-13

FIRST LESSON: HOSEA 5:15—6:6

In the collect for this Sunday, the church prays: "Forgive our disobedience . . .". These words capture in a nutshell the thrust of Hos.
5:15—6:6.

As his speeches attest, Hosea, a prophet of the kingdom of Israel
(750–721 B.C.), was unsurpassed in the passion with which he an-
nounced both the wrath that God would visit upon Israel because of
its unfaithfulness and the fervent love with which God desired that
Israel should repent and turn to him in faith and devotion (see chap.
2). Against the background of this pervasive theme of wrath and love,
5:15—6:6 presupposes a specific historical crisis, the Syro-Ephraimite
War (734–732 B.C.; 2 Kings 16:1-9).

Unimpressed by the power of Tiglath-pileser, Pekah, king of Israel,
joined forces with Rezin, king of Syria, to resist Assyrian domination.
To lend strength to their coalition, the two partners called on Ahaz,
king of Judah, to throw in with them. When Ahaz balked, Pekah and
Rezin set about to conquer Judah and depose Ahaz. Before they could
make good on their intentions, however, Tiglath-pileser attacked Israel
and reduced it to a rump state. Sensing opportunity in this, Ahaz,
too, attacked Israel and seized border territory for Judah.

Through Hosea, his mouthpiece, God addresses this situation. Announcing punishment, he excoriates Judah for seizing territory from
Israel (5:10) and Israel for forming a coalition with Syria (5:11). Then
comes the Old Testament lesson. In the opening verse, God suddenly
declares that he will withdraw from Israel and Judah (5:15). His absence, God muses, will cause them to recognize that the woes they
suffer are the result of their sins. Chastened, they will turn to him in
repentance and submit to him as the Lord.

In 6:1-3, we have a song of penitence. The question is how to interpret it. Does it constitute a sincere expression of remorse on the part of Israel and Judah? Or do Israel and Judah rather offer it as a cry of expediency calculated to induce God to rescue them from the ills besetting them?

The church has traditionally understood this song as a sincere expression of remorse on the part of Israel and Judah. This is also the position of the RSV and NRSV. At the end of 5:15, the RSV follows the Septuagint and adds the word *saying*. The result is that God is the one who sings this song and the song itself is illustrative of how Israel and Judah will seek God in their distress. The NRSV achieves the same result more economically, by simply ending v. 15 with a colon.

If the preacher chooses this option, then a sermon based on 5:15—6:6 becomes a straightforward call to repentance. In developing such a sermon, the preacher will find rich resources in Hosea for drawing analogies between the world of ancient Israel and Judah and our world today. Just as that world was torn by social, political, and religious crises, so our world is caught up in the same sort of turmoil. And just as Israel and Judah acknowledged their guilt and looked to God for deliverance, so we confess our sins and look to God for healing.

The alternative is to understand the song of penitence as a cry of expediency, the way the NJB views it. By ending 5:15 with a period, the NJB ascribes the song not to God but to Israel and Judah. As uttered by them, this song assumes the character of a quick fix: The appeal of Israel and Judah to God springs not from a repentant heart but from the desire to win reprieve from the calamities they suffer.

This interpretation of the song takes its cue from 6:4. Here God laments that the remorse of Israel and Judah is like the morning mist: It evaporates as soon as the sun strikes it. If one reads 6:1-3 in terms of 6:4, one sees how readily the words of the song express a desire on the part of Israel and Judah to manipulate God into serving their interests.

If the preacher opts for this construal of the song of penitence, the resultant sermon will likewise be a call to repentance, but by reverse example. The reason the congregation is now summoned to repentance is that there is a strong tendency in all of us to make light of our transgressions or indeed not even to see them. Judah and Israel not only do not repent of their sins but they also delude themselves into believing that through their empty words, they can manipulate God.

The blindness of Israel and Judah to their true condition impels us to examine penitentially our true condition.

The final word God speaks through Hosea is climactic (6:6). The act of repentance, God says in effect, is not merely a negative exercise but, positively, results in the steadfast love and knowledge of him. In the thought of Hosea, to love God steadfastly is to be single-hearted in one's devotion to him, and to have knowledge of God is to rely on him for one's salvation and to be obedient to him in life. In other words, through repentance God shapes both faith and life.

SECOND LESSON: ROMANS 4:18-25

In most sermons, preachers deal not so much with faith itself as with the various aspects of the Christian life it engenders. Romans 4:18-25 provides the preacher with a welcome opportunity to break routine and focus on the nature of faith.

In 4:18-25, Paul holds up Abraham as the exemplar who shows Christians what faith is and how it is exercised. In the three sections preceding this text, Paul discusses the faith of Abraham in relation to works (4:1-8), circumcision (4:9-12), and the inheritance of the promise given him (4:13-17). A brief review of the latter texts will enrich our understanding of the former.

In Romans 1–3, Paul has argued that God justifies—places in a right relationship with him—all people, whether Jew or gentile, by grace through faith in Jesus Christ without the works of the law (3:21-28). This emphasis on faith has left Paul with a problem: If it is by faith that one is justified, what becomes of works and the viability of the law (3:28-31)? This question is one Paul could not avoid, for Jewish contemporaries claimed that Abraham kept the law before it was even given.

To answer this question and also to insist on the centrality of faith in the history of God's dealings with Israel and humankind, Paul turns his attention in chapter 4 to Abraham, the father of Israel. In vv. 1-8, the question is whether or not Abraham was justified by works. He was not, Paul contends, and Scripture proves it. If one looks at Gen. 15:6, one discovers that God accounted Abraham as righteous not because of anything Abraham did, but because Abraham believed God. In vv. 9-12, the question is whether or not one's justification depends on observing the rite of circumcision; after all, Abraham observed this rite and the law commands it. Again, Paul's answer is negative. Just as Gen. 15:6 precedes Gen. 17:10, so one sees that in the historical life of Abraham, God justified him by faith before ever commanding him to observe the rite of circumcision. In vv. 13-17, the question is whether or not the heirs of the promise God gave Abraham are those who observe the law. Paul avers, By no means! God gave Abraham the promise at the very time he accounted him as righteous on the basis of faith (Gen. 15:5-6; Sir. 44:21). Hence, those who are heirs of Abraham's promise are not merely those who observe the law but all people who trust God in the way Abraham trusted him.

Having thus discussed Abraham's faith in relation to these three topics, Paul is now prepared, in 4:18-25, to define faith and to describe how Abraham exercised it. What is faith? Faith is to trust God completely that he will do what he says. For Abraham, faith was trusting God to make him the father of many nations (v. 18). For us, faith is trusting God that through the death and resurrection of Jesus Christ we stand in a right relationship with him so that we live under his lordship and lead lives that have meaning and purpose (vv. 23-25).

How is faith exercised? In the freedom it brings. Because he trusted God, Abraham was free to cherish the hope that God would make of him the father of many nations (4:18), to be unconcerned that he and Sarah were too old to have children (4:19), to give glory to God for the promise that, on the surface, seemed incapable of fulfillment (4:20), and to live in the quiet confidence that with God, nothing is impossible (4:21).

In the pulpit, the preacher might well wish to follow the contours of this text by both defining for the congregants what faith is and elaborating on the freedom faith brings. The latter point is important because we Christians often live as though we have no faith, refusing to let God be God. In trusting God that he has justified us in Jesus Christ, we find freedom to give our attention to the possibilities of life that lie within our reach, not to its great impossibilities that lie beyond us. In trusting God that our future is secure with him, we find freedom in the present to serve him and others. In trusting God that he is Lord of our lives, we find the freedom not to make ourselves the center of our own universe. And in trusting God that he is Lord of creation and history, we find the freedom to work for the welfare of creation and for the public good. Faith brings freedom, the freedom to experience the joy of living as a creature and child of God.

GOSPEL: MATTHEW 9:9-13

In the church today, the question of where to mark off moral and religious boundaries is a burning one. In Matt. 9:9-13, Jesus' act of eating with toll collectors and sinners touches on this very question.

A glance at 9:9-13 shows that it is a composite of two smaller pericopes. In v. 9, Matthew tells of the call of Matthew, the toll collector. In vv. 10-13, Matthew tells of the debate Jesus has with the Pharisees because he dares to have table fellowship with toll collectors and sinners.

These two pericopes relate to each other as "introduction" and "body." The significance of Jesus' call of the toll collector Matthew is that he summons to discipleship not one who is good and upright—like Peter, Andrew, James, or John—but one who is a social and religious outcast (9:9). This call of Matthew, therefore, serves as a fitting introduction to the pericope on Jesus' debate with the Pharisees, for this pericope depicts a scene in which Jesus reclines at table with many such outcasts as Matthew (9:10).

Seeing Jesus at table with outcasts, the Pharisees take umbrage at this (9:11). In their eyes, Jesus violates social and religious boundaries that must not only be maintained but even strengthened. In their display of anger, the Pharisees are acting out of profound conviction. For them, to have table fellowship is to participate in an act of great religious significance. Mealtime is an opportunity, amidst the routine of everyday life, to attest to the truth that Israel is God's holy people set apart to do his will. To make this attestation, one reclines at table in the same state of ritual purity as the priests in the temple. Conversely, to eat with such ritually and morally impure persons as toll collectors and sinners is to render oneself ritually impure. To the Pharisees' way of thinking, Jesus, in partaking of food with toll collectors and sinners, has publicly thumbed his nose at their religious custom and wantonly defiled himself.

Jesus views the situation differently. In him, God's rule is a present reality (12:28). By inviting social and religious outcasts to recline with him at table, he intends to extend God's love to them: He proffers them forgiveness, summons them to discipleship, and invites them to live in the sphere of God's rule. As Jesus himself declares: It is God's desire that he be merciful (9:13). Consequently, as the bearer of God's kingdom, Jesus radically redraws the very social boundaries the Pharisees are so intent on keeping intact. Inevitably, therefore, Jesus clashes with the Pharisees. To shock them into changing their mind, he lashes out at them with a scathing retort, "I have not come to call [those like you who think themselves to be] righteous, but [those who know themselves to be] sinners" (9:13).

This debate between Jesus and the Pharisees over "where to draw the boundaries" is one that is not unknown to the church today. Throughout the church, two sides have seemingly lined up against each other, and each side has its vocal extremists. The extremists on the one side are more akin to the Pharisees Matthew has described in the text. They have hard and fast views about Christian morality, about where the boundaries are, and they are at work to see to it that the church upholds these views. They believe that the church is known by its distinctiveness, and that if it is not resolutely vigilant about maintaining boundaries, it will forfeit its integrity and lose its identity. The watchword of this side is moral rigor, keeping the score, knowing who is "in" and who is "out."

The extremists on the other side constitute a caricature of Matthew's presentation of Jesus. In the name of love, they are prepared to redraw the moral and religious boundaries of the church in the interest of forging an accommodation with popular trends in society. They tend to have little to say about sin and repentance and think of love in terms of unqualified acceptance. Their watchword is openness, and they would have the church be open to the prevailing morality of the culture.

In the text, Jesus challenges the church to be discerning of moral and religious boundaries. On the one hand, Jesus himself redraws boundaries, but in light of the presence of God's rule and therefore in accordance with God's will. On the other hand, Jesus does not simply do away with boundaries. In having table fellowship with toll collectors and sinners, he extends God's love to them by summoning them to repentance and therefore to a life that comports itself with God's rule. To discern where to mark the boundaries is never easy. The church, however, has resources: The Spirit of Jesus, Scripture, and tradition.

Fourth Sunday after Pentecost

Lutheran	Roman Catholic	Episcopal	Common Lectionary
Exod. 19:2-8a	Exod. 19:2-6a	Exod. 19:2-8a	Gen. 25:19-34
Rom. 5:6-11	Rom. 5:6-11	Rom. 5:6-11	Rom. 5:6-11
Matt. 9:35—10:8	Matt. 9:36—10:8	Matt. 9:35—10:8	Matt. 9:35—10:8

FIRST LESSON: EXODUS 19:2-8a

Exodus 19:6a is directly quoted by the author of 1 Pet. (2:9). In preparing a sermon on 19:2-8a, the preacher should consider pairing it with 1 Pet. 2:4-10. Both texts highlight the theme of election: that of Israel on the one hand and that of the church on the other. In a society made up of a blizzard of groups and organizations—civic, social, educational, business, labor, military, charitable, environmental, ethnic—the church is continually enticed to think of itself as simply one more association of like-minded people who, in this case, happen to be dedicated to spiritual matters and moral betterment. This is especially the case with Protestants, who tend to regard the individual congregation as autonomous and not much different from the local PTA or civic association. To correct this false image of the church, a sermon on election can be an effective first step.

Exodus 19:2-8a tells of God's appearance to Israel on Mount Sinai, at which time God makes a covenant with Israel (vv. 3, 5). In entering into this covenant, God elects Israel to be his people. In its outward form, God's covenant with Israel resembles the ancient suzerainty treaty (vv. 4-8a). In such a treaty, the ruler, after citing the benevolent acts he has performed on behalf of the vassal, binds the vassal to him in a relationship in which the vassal responds to him not out of coercion but out of gratitude.

In line with this treaty form, God announces in v. 4 that the covenant he makes with Israel rests on his initiative: Just as an eagle will carry its young on outstretched wings, so God has brought Israel out of Egypt to himself at Sinai. The emphasis here is on God's grace. God does not choose Israel because it is more numerous, powerful, beautiful, or noble than other nations, but solely because of his unmerited love.

Israel, in fact, is little more than a band of wretched slaves. This notwithstanding, God elects Israel to be "my treasured possession" among all peoples (v. 5), to be a "kingdom of priests" and a "holy nation" (v. 6). To be God's own possession is to be a people devoted to him and to him alone. To be a kingdom of priests is to be the people among whom God dwells. And to be a holy nation is to be a people consecrated, or set apart, for God's service. In response to God's words, Israel endorses the covenant by replying in one voice, "Everything that the LORD has spoken we will do" (v. 8a).

The author of 1 Peter wrote toward the end of the first century to gentile Christians living in the northern provinces of Asia Minor (1:1). Not unlike Israel at Sinai, these Christians apparently belonged to the lower classes and were perhaps laborers and slaves. As Christians, they no longer participated in pagan rites; as a result, they lived isolated in their communities and were the object of slander and sporadic persecutions (4:16). The author's purpose in writing these Christians was to encourage them to remain steadfast in faith and not to weaken (5:12).

In 2:4-10, the author holds up to these ragtag Christians an exalted picture of who they really are: the elect of God. The author stresses that though they live as aliens in this world, they are in reality "a chosen race," "a royal priesthood," "a holy nation," and "God's own people" (v. 9). Because of the unmerited mercy God has shown them (v. 10), they have faith in Jesus Christ (v. 7), who is God's Elect (v. 6). Through their faith in God's Elect, they have become the elect of God (v. 9), God's covenant people. As God's elect, they inherit the exalted names of Israel, which proclaim their identity and significance. Thus, they are "a royal priesthood," for God dwells among them. They are "a holy nation," for God has consecrated them by his Holy Spirit for his service. And they are "God's own people," for they are distinct from the world and special to him. As the elect, covenant people of God, their task is to proclaim to the world "God's mighty acts," which is to say that they are to announce what God has done in Jesus Christ to call all people out of darkness and to enlighten them (v. 9).

It may have been true in the past that the church thought more highly of itself than it ought. Today, however, the danger is the reverse. In expositing texts on election, the preacher reminds the church of what it means to be the end time people of God.

SECOND LESSON: ROMANS 5:1-11

Like "justification," "reconciliation" is one of those five-dollar words that is often used in the pulpit but is seldom defined. Along with 2 Cor. 5:17-20, Rom. 5:10-11 is the key passage in which Paul explicates his understanding of reconciliation. In the epistle for this Sunday, Paul asserts that because we have been justified by God—or indeed reconciled to him—through Jesus Christ, we have reason to boast, but only in God.

In 5:1-11, Paul takes up two questions that he anticipates the Christians at Rome are eager to ask of him: Is it not true that the sufferings we must endure disprove the claim that we have been justified by God (vv. 1-5)? And what about our sins? Do they not disprove the gospel of justification (vv. 6-11)?

In 5:1-5, Paul answers the question about suffering. In doing so, he does not argue but assumes that through the death of Jesus Christ, we Christians have in fact been justified and stand in a right relationship with God (v. 1). By virtue of this, we presently live in the sphere of God's grace and we boast in the sure hope that God will, at the last judgment, grant us salvation (v. 2). Do our sufferings, then, disprove our justification and our hope of final salvation? Not at all, Paul contends; they rather strengthen our hope. Suffering produces endurance, the quality of persevering in faith to the end (v. 3). Endurance produces character, the quality of having one's faith tested and found genuine (v. 4). Character produces hope, the quality of having one's expectation of final salvation strengthened as one's faith is put to the test (v. 4). And hope will never disappoint us. Why not? Because it is real and not a mere figment of our imagination. How do we know this? Because God has given us the gift of his Spirit and thus attested to his great love for us (v. 5).

In 5:6-11, Paul replies to the question about our sins. Does the fact that we Christians are sinners disprove the truth that God has justified us? Not at all, Paul declares, for Jesus' death is unlike that of any other human who has ever lived. From human experience, we know how rare it is that anyone should lay down his or her life for another person (v. 7). In contrast, look at Christ. At a time when we were neither "upright" nor "truly good" but "weak"—ungodly sinners to be exact— God demonstrated his love for us by justifying us through the death of Christ (vv. 6, 8). Now since God has already accomplished this infinitely difficult feat of justifying us while we were ungodly, we can be all the more certain that he will save us from condemnation at the latter day (v. 9).

Indeed, Paul continues, one can speak of this phenomenon of justification more personally, in terms of "reconciliation" (5:10-11). Formerly, we were enemies of God and hostile toward him (v. 10). While we were still his enemies, however, God in Christ reconciled us to himself, which is to say that he did away with all hostilities and bestowed on us the gift of peace (vv. 1, 10). Since to bestow the gift of peace on enemies is an infinitely difficult thing to do, how much easier will it not be for God, now that he has made us his friends, to grant us salvation at the end of the age (v. 10)? In wonderment at all this, we even boast, yet our boasting is strictly in God, based on Christ's reconciling death (v. 11).

In working through 5:1-11, the preacher will have noted that Paul speaks of "boasting" both at the beginning and end (vv. 2-3, 11). As Paul uses this word, it bears the positive meaning of "rejoicing" (RSV). Still, earlier in Romans Paul used "boasting" in a negative sense, as he made the point that the Jew, no more than the gentile, can presume that he stands in a favored relationship with God (2:17-24). In taking the "Jew" to task for boasting, Paul is not being anti-Semitic. No, Paul takes the Jew to task because, in his view, if there is any human who might have a right to boast, it is the Jew, for the Jew epitomizes religion at its best.

In thus dealing with the Jew, Paul touches on something that goes to the very core of human nature. Deeply ingrained in all of us is the notion that if God is to be gracious toward us, it will be only because we have something whereof to boast, some quality we possess or some deed we perform. At a refined level, this quality or deed is usually thought of as faith. On the lips of many pulpiteers, the familiar words, "If only we believe, God will be gracious toward us," subtly take on the sense of "Because we believe . . . ". More crassly, some make not only faith but also any number of dos and don'ts the precondition for receiving God's grace. In point of fact, we humans should scarcely be surprised that we find inside us the elemental feeling that we dare never stand in the presence of God without having something with which to make us acceptable to him. For us to be told that God is gracious toward us for nothing makes us suspicious. For us to be told that we must earn God's grace is something we readily understand.

Throughout Romans, however, Paul insists time and again that while we were yet sinners, God in Christ reconciled us to himself. Have we, then, reason to boast? Yes, but only in God, on account of Christ.

GOSPEL: MATTHEW 9:35—10:8

In the Gospel for this Sunday, Jesus commissions the twelve disciples to a ministry in Israel. As could be expected in a scene like this, Jesus occupies center stage as a towering figure of authority. Standing before Jesus are the Twelve, and they, too, have the appearance of being larger than life: They are portrayed as power-laden individuals commissioned to accomplish extraordinary things. Still, attractive as this image is, it is one-sided and only partially describes the disciples as Matthew would have them seen. As we shall discover, Matthew wants the disciples to be seen not as invincible heroes but as frail humans whom Jesus empowers to undertake a ministry that serves as an extension of his own. In other words, first impressions notwithstanding, the disciples in the text are much like the Christians of Matthew's church must have been or, for that matter, much as we are.

Matthew is at pains to present the ministry of the Twelve to Israel as an extension of Jesus' own ministry. Jesus himself, Matthew points out, has been traversing the whole of Galilee teaching, preaching, and healing (9:35). Regardless, the numbers of people he has yet to reach are like a vast harvest waiting to be reaped (9:37). Also, urgency is the order of the day, for the religious authorities have failed the people and the latter are like endangered sheep that have no shepherd (9:36).

In the face of such danger and opportunity, Jesus summons the twelve disciples (10:1). To make it unmistakably clear that they go out as his ambassadors, he does three things. First, he grants to them authority and hence shows that they do not act on their own (10:1). Just as God endowed him with authority at his baptism, so Jesus now shares this authority with the disciples. Second, Jesus momentarily steps aside so that Matthew can cite the names of the disciples (10:2-4). The purpose of this ritual is to indicate that the circle of the Twelve is now closed and that the Twelve are now ready for ministry. Third, in commissioning the disciples, Jesus sends them to the same people to whom he has gone and enjoins them to do the same things he has done (10:5b-8). Just as Jesus declares to the Canaanite woman that he has been sent only to the "lost sheep of the house of Israel" (15:24), so he sends the disciples to the "lost sheep of the house of Israel" (10:6). And just as Jesus has proclaimed the nearness of the kingdom and healed (4:17; chaps. 8–9), so the disciples are to proclaim the nearness of the kingdom and to heal (10:7-8).

Thus far, we have focused on the heroic side of Matthew's picture of the disciples: In the authority they possess and the ministry they discharge, they are "Jesus-like." But Matthew also wants us to see them in another light: as frail humans. To lend balance to his picture, Matthew deftly incorporates two notations into the list of the disciples' names. After "Matthew," he writes, "the toll collector" (10:3). And after "Judas Iscariot," he writes, "who also betrayed him" (10:4). Though Matthew, the toll collector, is a disciple of Jesus, in the public eye he retains the image of a tax officer, one who is hated and despised by fellow Jews. And the notation about Judas quickly calls to mind a fixed set of events that later takes place: Judas betrays Jesus, Peter denies him, and all the disciples forsake him. Though Jesus-like in the authority and ministry entrusted to them, the disciples remain frail humans.

Frail humans that we Christians know ourselves to be, the risen Jesus has also commissioned us to a ministry that is an extension of his earthly ministry. After the manner of the Twelve, the risen Jesus has commissioned and empowered us, as at the time of our baptism, to a ministry to the shepherdless of society, to the morally and religiously helpless and harassed. One need not be clairvoyant to perceive the moral and religious confusion that hangs as a pall over our society. As poll after poll shows, people sense that "traditional values" are steadily eroding and that not all is well with society. People hunger for spiritual guidance. To satisfy this hunger, there is no lack of religious hucksters and self-proclaimed spiritual experts who are eager to become shepherds to these people. As perhaps never before, therefore, people need to hear from frail, yet Jesus-like Christians the gracious words of the gospel of the kingdom and to receive the ministrations that will heal them in body and spirit. As Jesus says in the text, "The harvest is plentiful!"

Fifth Sunday after Pentecost

Lutheran	Roman Catholic	Episcopal	Common Lectionary
Jer. 20:7-13	Jer. 20:10-13	Jer. 20:7-13	Gen. 28:10-17
Rom. 5:12-15	Rom. 5:12-15	Rom. 5:15b-19	Rom. 5:12-19
Matt. 10:24-33	Matt. 10:26-33	Matt. 10:24-33	Matt. 10:24-33

FIRST LESSON: JEREMIAH 20:7-13

Politics, as the old adage goes, is the art of compromise. In a pluralistic society, this adage not only seems to have a special ring of truth about it but it also seems reasonable to apply it not just to politics but to all areas of life. But when does practicing the art of compromise result in one's losing one's integrity? This is a question the Old Testament lesson addresses.

Jeremiah, a prophet of the kingdom of Judah, was active during the four decades preceding the kingdom's demise (626–587 B.C.). The world in which Jeremiah prophesied was one of political turmoil and shifting alliances. Assyria was in eclipse as a world power, Babylon was in the ascendancy, and Egypt was eager to shore up Assyria at the expense of Babylon. Living at the edge of the storm, Judah was, sequentially, independent, an enemy and then ally of Egypt, and a vassal of Babylon. During Jeremiah's ministry, the burning question Judah faced concerned the foreign policy it should pursue to secure its future.

This question divided Judah's leaders into two opposing factions. The larger faction, comprising prophets, priests, nobles, and royalty, argued that Judah's future lay in its autonomy and that Babylon should be resisted. The smaller faction, which was also made up of prophets, priests, and influential nobility, was the one to which Jeremiah belonged. As Jeremiah saw it, Judah's future lay in not resisting Babylon. Not Babylonian hegemony but Judah's lust for false gods and unfaithfulness to the true God was the real threat it had to meet if it were to survive as a nation.

The immediate background for understanding 20:7-13 is the symbolic act Jeremiah performs in chapter 19 and the subsequent persecution he has to endure (10:1-6). At God's command, Jeremiah purchases an earthenware jug, goes to the Potsherd Gate that opens out onto the valley of Hinnom, and announces that disaster will befall Judah because of its unfaithfulness to God. To symbolize the ruination of Judah, Jeremiah breaks the jug. To provoke his enemies even more, he walks to the temple and there condemns Judah as an obdurate people that steadfastly refuses to obey God. Unamused by Jeremiah's pronouncements, Pashhur, a priest and chief officer of the temple, beats Jeremiah and has him held up to public ridicule by throwing him in the stocks. Released the next day, Jeremiah promptly attacks Pashhur, renaming him "Terror-all-around," and predicts, along with the destruction of Judah, his death in exile.

Under the burden of these experiences, Jeremiah retreats momentarily and cries out to God in a soul-wrenching lament (20:7-13). Almost blasphemously, he complains that God has seduced and forced him into announcing Judah's destruction (vv. 7-9). In fact, so often has he bewailed Judah's fate that the people have derisively nicknamed him "Terror-all-around" (v. 10). Whereas friends watch to see if he will stumble, his enemies plot revenge (v. 10). Truly, his prophetic office has earned him nothing but contempt.

At this juncture, the black mood of Jeremiah's lament suddenly changes to one of confidence. In praise of God, Jeremiah expresses his trust that though God has seen fit sorely to test him, he does not doubt that God will see after his protection and cause his enemies to fail (vv. 11-12).

If these scenes are any indication, they suggest that one thought that never crossed Jeremiah's mind was that he should enter into compromise with his opponents or accommodate his message to society's prevailing views. In fact, the career of Jeremiah stands as testimony to the truth that there are indeed areas of life in which integrity demands that one not practice the art of compromise and accommodation. In this respect, Jeremiah may be regarded as the predecessor of those two great figures to come, Jesus and Paul. When it came to matters of faith and life, Jesus and Paul, too, were never ones to rush headlong to society's negotiating table.

At home in a pluralistic society, the church is under continual pressure to accommodate its faith and life to society's shifting norms. As the church responds to this pressure, integrity demands that it take as firm a stand as a Jeremiah while at the same time avoiding two extremes. The one extreme is that the church declare matters to be non-negotiable that in reality are nonessential. If the church does this, it unnecessarily shuts itself off from society. The other extreme is that the church declare matters to be nonessential that in reality belong to the fundamentals of its faith and life. If the church does this, it forfeits its integrity and becomes unfaithful to its God and Lord. Times today are as fluid as they were in Jeremiah's Judah. During such times, it is critical that the church knows both where it stands and what it stands for.

SECOND LESSON: ROMANS 5:12-19

The popular notion of free will is distinctly modern. It construes individuals as autonomous beings who have the luxury of standing in a moral and religious neutral zone and choosing which god, if any, they will serve and what kind of lives they will lead. Such a notion would cause Paul and his contemporaries to blink in utter disbelief. For ancients such as Paul, the world was not thought of as a place filled with morally autonomous individuals but as a place that is not only home to humans but is also abuzz with supernatural forces that are good and evil, personal and impersonal, and that exercise varying degrees of authority: principalities, powers, gods, spirits, angels, and demons. Because humans are necessarily subject to the influence of such forces, the ancients were vitally concerned to ask about their nature and intentions.

In Rom. 5:12-19, Paul touches on this critical issue by comparing Adam with Christ. Adam for Paul is both the first human being, who is the father of the human race, and the universal human being, who is the head of a fallen humanity. Christ is both the earthly human being, who was perfectly obedient to God, and the heavenly human being, who is the head of a new humanity.

In drawing this comparison between Adam and Christ, Paul understands Adam both to be analogous to Christ and to contrast with Christ. Adam is analogous to Christ in the sense that the actions of each have affected the whole of humanity. Adam contrasts with Christ in the sense that the effect each has had on the whole of humanity is diametrically opposite.

Paul's extended analogy and contrast run like this. (a) Just as Adam disobeyed God (Gen. 2:17: "Of the tree of the knowledge of good and evil you shall not eat"), so all of us humans have disobeyed God (5:19). Just like Adam, so all of us, because of our disobedience, have fallen under the power of sin (5:12). Just like Adam, so all of us, because of our sin, stand condemned before God (5:16, 18). And just like Adam, so all of us, because we stand condemned, have become subject to death (5:12, 17). (*b*) Unlike Adam, Christ was obedient to God (5:19). Unlike Adam, Christ, throughout his life, stood in a right relationship with God (5:18). Unlike Adam, Christ brought justification, that is to say, he brought all of us into a right relationship with God (5:16, 18). And unlike Adam, Christ proffers to all of us the gift of eternal life (5:17-18).

Accordingly, in 5:12-19 Paul, through the vehicle of analogy and contrast, describes humanity "in Adam," the universal human being, and "in Christ," the heavenly human being. In Adam, humanity exists in alienation from God: It is disobedient to God, lives under the power of sin, stands condemned before God, and reaps the punishment of death. In Christ, humanity is the recipient of the grace of God: It stands in a right relationship with God and has the gift of eternal life.

In terms of the modern notion of free will, the thrust of Paul's argument in 5:12-19 is that this notion is a chimera. There is no human being in the world who is morally or religiously autonomous. We all serve some master. What is more, the multiplicity of masters we think we serve can all, ultimately, be reduced to two: People either serve sin and live alienated from God, or they serve Christ and live in a right relationship with God. The end result of serving sin is death; the end result of serving Christ is life eternal. Thanks be to God: It is Christ who is the Lord of our lives!

GOSPEL: MATTHEW 10:24-33

If one half of the hermeneutical circle consists in determining the central message of the text, then Matt. 10:24-33 will, in this respect, cause the preacher little difficulty: In vv. 24-33, Jesus summons the disciples to be utterly fearless in bearing public witness to him. Still, easy as it may be to determine the central message of vv. 24-33, the preacher may well find that negotiating the second half of the hermeneutical circle and turning the message of vv. 24-33 into a word from God for people today will require both thought and imagination.

To elaborate the message of 10:24-33, it neatly unfolds in line with the text's structure. (*a*) In vv. 24-25, Jesus declares that the disciples are to be like him, which is to say that they, too, will meet with persecution (see 9:34). (*b*) In vv. 26-29, Jesus three times exhorts the disciples "not to fear." They are not to fear, for it is God's will that they proclaim boldly and publicly what Jesus has revealed to them in private (vv. 26-27). They are not to fear, for although their enemies have the power to kill them, such power cannot be compared to God's power to visit on humans eternal punishment (v. 28). And they are not to fear, for if God watches over such insignificant creatures as sparrows, how much more will he watch over the disciples, whom he values infinitely more (vv. 29-31). (c) In vv. 32-33, Jesus caps this sequence of sayings by enjoining the disciples to bear public witness to him in the confidence that, at the latter day, he will acknowledge before God those who acknowledge him now.

To consider 10:24-33 as a word for people today, the question the preacher confronts is how to proclaim it so that congregants will perceive it as touching them in their own situation. Perhaps the most obvious way to proclaim it is to draw an analogy between the situation of Matthew's church and the situation of Christians today. True, the situation in which Matthew's church found itself was extreme: Apparently, disciples who bore fearless witness to Christ had to reckon with persecution and even the loss of life. By contrast, Christians who bear witness to their faith in Western society need not fear overt persecution because they enjoy the protection of law.

Still, to say this can be misleading: In many sectors of the Western world and of the United States, open witness to Christian faith—even that of the best kind—not only is not welcome but meets with suspicion, resistance, ridicule, or hostility. One reason for this is that the influence of Christianity has waned considerably in the last decades and will presumably continue to do so. The old canard that the United States is a "Christian nation," though it was never correct, is nonetheless scarcely heard anymore. In certain quarters, people look at Christianity with a jaundiced eye and view it as an enemy of freedom and the personification of intolerance and bigotry. Solemn Christian feasts, such as Christmas and Easter, have become almost completely secularized. In both learned papers and popular books, cultured intellectuals contend that ours is now a "post-Christian" era. For the church to survive, some well-intentioned Christians call for it to circle the wagons and radically mark itself off from the rest of society. While some may applaud these trends and other deplore them, the point is this: In a society that prides itself on being radically pluralistic, to bear open witness to Christ is regarded as being at odds with the public good. The upshot is that

Christians who do attest openly to their faith do in fact meet with subtle or not so subtle forms of persecution. At first blush, then, the preacher may have thought it ludicrous to preach 10:24-33 in such fashion as to draw an analogy between the situation of Matthew's church and that of his or her own congregation. In reality, however, for the preacher to summon the congregants to bear fearless witness to Christ in the face of mounting public opposition is no mean thing.

A second way to preach 10:24-33 is to take a different tack and to focus on the question, "In today's society, how can we Christians best bear public witness to Christ?" In the United States, ours is a society that thinks of religion as a purely private matter that has no role to play in the public sector. The result is that, whether for good or for ill, such acts as praying or confessing one's faith are held to be out of place in the classroom, the boardroom, the workshop, or city hall. We Christians may worship in church on Sunday, but from Monday through Friday we live, work, and study in a secularized world.

Given this situation, is there any possible way that we can act on the injunction of 10:24-33 to bear fearless witness to Christ in public? Indirectly, there is such a way. Earlier in Matthew's Gospel, Jesus said, "You will know them by their fruits" (7:16, 20); and throughout his Gospel, Matthew holds Jesus up as the model the disciples are to emulate in their lives. In other words, Matthew places great store in his Gospel by the power of example. And so must we Christians today. By the power of our example, we can acknowledge Christ before others and show that we are his disciples. And by the power of our example, we can invite others to inquire after our witness to Christ. When others do so inquire, we will stand ready to speak both lovingly and fearlessly of the Lord we confess and serve.

Sixth Sunday after Pentecost

Lutheran	Roman Catholic	Episcopal	Common Lectionary
Jer. 28:5-9	2 Kings 4:8-11, 14-16a	Isa. 2:10-17	Gen. 32:22-32
Rom. 6:1b-11	Rom. 6:3-4, 8-11	Rom. 6:3-11	Rom. 6:3-11
Matt. 10:34-42	Matt. 10:37-42	Matt. 10:34-42	Matt. 10:34-42

FIRST LESSON: JEREMIAH 28:5-9

In recent years, the church has recognized anew the need to speak a prophetic word amid the maelstrom of society's trends and struggles. Nowadays, preachers aim to proclaim a prophetic word from the pulpit, congregants look to hear a prophetic word, and church boards and commissions intend for their papers and reports to contain a prophetic word. But how are preachers, boards, or congregants to know that the word they announce or hear is in fact prophetic? What are the marks of the prophetic word? Jeremiah 28:5-9 suggests some clues to look for.

In many cases, words that masquerade as prophetic but are in reality hollow are as easy to spot as a three-dollar bill. Preachers, evangelists, commissions, or institutions that promote a cause in the name of the Lord so as to enhance their own prestige and power or to pad wallet or budget fool no one. No, the difficulty arises when a word that invokes divine authority and summons the faithful in all sincerity and conviction to do the will of God is nonetheless counterfeit and leads people astray.

This is the situation we have in Jeremiah's clash with Hananiah. Both Jeremiah and Hananiah are certified prophets (28:5). Both address the people in the temple, Israel's central shrine (28:2, 5). Both claim that they speak in the name of God ("Thus says the Lord"; 28:2, 11, 16). And both are convinced that the message they proclaim announces the will of God (27:16-22; 28:2-4).

Yet the message of Hananiah is the exact opposite of that of Jeremiah. The year is 594 B.C. and Babylon is at the height of its power. Under King Zedekiah, Judah, though a vassal of Babylon, has become restless. Speaking on behalf of the nation's dominant party, Hananiah counsels

41

resistance against Babylon on the grounds that God will break Babylon's yoke of domination (28:2-4). For his part, Jeremiah counsels submission to Babylon and prayer to God that God may yet spare Judah from the certain destruction that will befall it if it persists in pursuing a policy of national independence (27:16-22).

Which prophet, then, is Judah to heed? Whose word is authentically prophetic and whose word is false? In deciding these questions, Jeremiah urges us in 28:5-9 to ponder several important factors. First, the true prophetic word is one that is spoken under the sign of repentance. In v. 8, Jeremiah places himself in the long line of Israel's prophets who did call the nation to repentance. In contrast, Hananiah promises Judah "cheap grace," peace without repentance. What this means, therefore, is that for the preacher who would announce and the congregation who would hear the prophetic word, repentance is the order of the day. In addition, this means that the local congregation, having itself received the word of forgiveness, does not ignore the sins of the nation. Indeed, the church dare never forget that it serves as a blessing to the nation when it invokes God for Christ's sake to show forbearance toward the nation and not to visit on it the consequences of its sins.

Second, the true prophetic word is one that assesses the present in the light of God's actions in the past. In v. 8, we note that Jeremiah, in aligning himself with the prophets before him, aligns his message with a tradition that measures the spiritual health of Israel, whether that of the kingdom of Israel or of Judah, in terms of its faithfulness to the God who elected it to be his chosen people. In the case of Hananiah, his message has no roots in Israel's tradition of redemption and election, for he conveniently overlooks Judah's idolatry and prophesies peace in the face of unfaithfulness (v. 9). As the church contemplates the tradition by which it measures the spiritual health of both itself and the nation, it identifies the salvation that God has accomplished in Jesus Christ as the foundational act that gives shape to this tradition. The prophetic word that the preacher proclaims and the congregation hears, therefore, is one that enjoins the church to conduct itself in the present in a way that comports itself with this salvation, which is also the kind of conduct that God wills for the nation.

Third, the true prophetic word is one that takes no delight in suffering and punishment. In response to Hananiah's cheerful message of future bliss, Jeremiah pronounces a firm "Amen!" and declares it his profoundest wish that Hananiah's words might prove true (v. 6). Hananiah, in turn, because he is blind to the prospect of Judah's ruin, cannot even appreciate what it might mean to long fervently for peace while at the same time perceiving the signs of approaching doom. As the preacher proclaims the prophetic word, he or she will search the heart to make certain that the prophetic word is spoken in love. The prophetic word tends to be a hard word, one that lays bare personal and national faults and calls for change. All the more, therefore, should the preacher be wary lest he or she, in proclaiming the prophetic word, heap guilt on others while at the same time donning a cloak of self-righteousness.

Last, the true prophetic word is one that can also envisage change and restoration. Having summoned Judah to no repentance, Hananiah's reassuring predictions are empty. Jeremiah, whose calls to repentance Judah will not hear, can nonetheless envisage Judah's restoration following its punishment (chap. 30). Strictly speaking, the preacher does not proclaim the prophetic word as an exercise in itself. Instead, the preacher proclaims and the congregation hears the prophetic word so that they might repent, and God, by the power of his Spirit, might effect change both in them and in the nation. Ultimately, therefore, the prophetic word aims not at punishment, but at wholeness and salvation.

SECOND LESSON: ROMANS 6:1b-11

As the pastor or priest well knows, preaching is a genre all its own. Though it informs, it is not the art of teaching or lecturing. Though it must be convincing, it is not the art of persuasion. And though it aims to stir people to action, it is not the art of salesmanship. Instead, preaching is proclaiming the gospel, the good news of the salvation God proffers to humans in Jesus Christ.

Simple as it is to define preaching, it is apparently not so simple, Sunday in and Sunday out, to proclaim the gospel. To convince oneself of this, one has only to visit a variety of congregations and take note of whether the gospel does in fact come to word in Sunday morning's sermon. All too often, sermons are interesting, rousing, touching, or clever, but because they fail to proclaim the gospel—the one thing necessary—they do not, strictly speaking, constitute Christian preaching.

The flip side of this is that congregants are made to endure an overabundance of moralizing. Too easily, the pulpit becomes a podium for analyzing moral and social problems and for exhorting congregants to action. To exhort congregants to action without proclaiming the gospel, however, is to leave them to the strength of their own spiritual resolve to lead the Christian life, something they cannot do. As the New Testament says throughout, it is only by God's grace in Christ that Christians walk in newness of life. In Rom. 6:1b-11 Paul makes this very point, which is one reason why this text is of such critical theological importance.

The declaration on which 6:1b-11 turns is found in v. 6, where Paul states that "our old self" has been crucified with Christ so that it "might be destroyed, and we might no longer be enslaved to sin." The theme Paul sounds is that of freedom: freedom from the power of sin (v. 7); and freedom to live for God (v. 10). How do we get free from the power of sin? By dying (v. 7), says Paul. How do we die? By participating in Christ's death and burial through immersion in the waters of baptism (vv. 3-4, 8a). Having died in baptism, we are beyond the control of sin and sin no longer enslaves us. Still, to die is but the negative side of obtaining freedom.

The positive side is to "walk in newness of life" (vv. 4, 11). Christ not only died, he was also raised from the dead by God (v. 4). The life Christ now lives, therefore, is resurrection life. For us, however, resurrection life remains a promise and a hope (vv. 5, 8). Not until the resurrection of the dead at the end of time will we attain to it. Still, the gift that the risen Christ even now bestows on us is the power to walk in newness of life (v. 4). Consequently, in the interim between having died with Christ in baptism and being raised to live with him, we are empowered by him to lead lives pleasing to God.

From this brief exposition, it is clear that Rom. 6:1b-11 is a parade example of how integrally Paul associates the newness of Christian life with the proclamation of the gospel. To Paul's way of thinking, the nexus between the gospel and newness of life is based on the fundamental truth that apart from the proclamation of the gospel, there can be no newness of life. By ourselves, we humans, Christians though we may be, do not have within us the moral and spiritual resources to make good on exhortations to lead the Christian life. The preacher may enjoin us to "be alive to God" (v. 11), but unless he or she delivers this injunction as a gospel imperative, that is, as an injunction that is grounded in the preaching of the gospel, it avails nothing. Exactly because the newness of Christian life depends on the gospel, the gospel necessarily becomes the distinguishing mark of the genre of preaching.

If the proclamation of the gospel is crucial to Christian preaching, why is it so frequently conspicuous in sermons by its absence? One possible answer is that preachers may find it difficult to speak in a fresh way each Sunday of what God has done for us in Jesus Christ. To analyze problems can be interesting, and to exhort the congregation can be stirring. But how can one preach the gospel each Sunday without becoming boring and monotonous? The answer is to observe the many ways in which the gospel is preached in the New Testament. To remind ourselves of some of these ways, it is preached as justification, reconciliation, expiation, redemption, liberation, atonement, and restoration. The gospel is the one power that enables the Christian life. Because sermon imperatives are gospel imperatives, the preacher will be at his or her best in discovering fresh ways to proclaim the gospel.

GOSPEL: MATTHEW 10:34-42

In the Gospel for this Sunday, the Matthean Jesus utters words about discipleship, allegiance, and reward that are tailored to address Christians living in a situation we can scarcely envisage. Today, one becomes a Christian by being born into the church or by publicly confessing one's faith and being baptized. In Matthew's environment, however, it was routine for one who became a Christian to pay a high social, personal, and religious price. When, therefore, Jesus describes himself in 10:34-36 as one who does not create peace but causes division, and like a sword, even severs members of a family from one another, the Christians of Matthew's church would already have known what he means. Similarly, when Jesus lays absolute claim in 10:37-39 to the allegiance of the disciples, declaring that they are to love him more than father, mother, son, or daughter and, in fact, be prepared to endure persecution and even death for him, the Christians of Matthew's church would have knowingly nodded assent. And when in 10:40-42 Jesus calls the disciples ambassadors of both himself and God and assures them that those who receive them on their missionary travels will themselves be rewarded at the last day, the Christians of Matthew's church would have taken courage from such promises.

Today, we hear these words of Jesus about discipleship, allegiance, and reward in a vastly different context. The context in which we live is not one of overt persecution but one marked by secularization and relativism. Although at its founding, America could be said to be a Christian nation in the sense that Christianity was the religion of the vast majority of its people, in the course of two centuries Christianity has lost much of its authority to command society's attention and assent. Add to this the determination of Americans to preserve a strict separation between church and state and the result is that as Christianity has become increasingly marginalized, American society in general has become increasingly secular. Along with this trend, the notion of truth in America has also undergone change: Just as the absolute truth ascribed to religion was superseded by the absolute truth ascribed to reason and science, so the absolute truth of the latter has given way to the notion that truth is fundamentally relative. At the present time, therefore, the context in which we hear Jesus' words in 10:34-42 is one in which Christianity has been marginalized, society is largely secular, and truth is thought to be a matter of opinion.

In awareness of this context, how shall the preacher proclaim this text? The heart of the matter is that Jesus summons us to give to him our total allegiance (10:37-39). Consequently, one tack the preacher might take is to point the congregants to the risen Jesus as the one to cling to and to emulate. Within the confines of the church sanctuary, the congregants fervently and without restraint confess Jesus as Lord. But come Monday morning, they live and work in a secular society in which materialism and relativism are the driving forces. In this atmosphere, success becomes the supreme measure of a person and truth is regarded not as anything remotely fixed but as something to be manipulated in the service of any particular idea or cause. To counteract these forces, the preacher will want to proclaim the text so that the congregants can hear Jesus summon them to find in him the center of their lives, to find in discipleship the measure of their worth, and to find in his words and deeds—God's revelation to his people—the norm of religious truth and the light by which they walk. God has not left his people alone in the world; sustaining them is Jesus Christ, the one who has overcome the world.

Seventh Sunday after Pentecost

Lutheran	Roman Catholic	Episcopal	Common Lectionary
Zech. 9:9-12	Zech. 9:9-10	Zech. 9:9-12	Exod. 1:6-14, 22—2:10
Rom. 7:15-25a	Rom. 8:9, 11-13	Rom. 7:21—8:6	Rom. 7:14-25a
Matt. 11:25-30	Matt. 11:25-30	Matt. 11:25-30	Matt. 11:25-30

FIRST LESSON: ZECHARIAH 9:9-12

In the Apostles' Creed, we confess that we believe in Jesus Christ who "will come again to judge the living and the dead." This is an alternative way of expressing the fervent hope found especially in the synoptic Gospels that Christ will one day return as king and establish God's universal rule in splendor. While it was Jesus' "first coming" that gave shape to this hope, its origins can be traced to Old Testament texts such as Zech. 9:9-12. In 9:9-12, the ancient prophet looks to the future and predicts that God will raise up a new Davidic king and establish his rule over the nations.

Zechariah 9:9-12 is situated in the second part of the book (chaps. 9–14). Whereas the first part encompasses chapters 1–8 and stems from the prophet Zechariah (520–518 B.C.), the second part originated with anonymous authors who were active sometime during the fifth and fourth centuries B.C. Whereas the first part largely contains visions pertaining to the restoration of God's chosen people, the second part contains two oracles that tell of divine judgment and salvation at the end of time (chaps. 9–11; 12–14). Although the situation in which 9:9-12 arose is difficult to discern, scholars speculate that it was one of extreme crisis. Having returned to Jerusalem from Babylon, the exiles faced communal problems so intractable that they turned to the future and hoped for God's direct intervention on their behalf.

The text itself falls into two parts: Verses 9-10 foretell the coming of a new Davidic king, and vv. 11-12 constitute an oracle of salvation. Of importance in vv. 9-10 is the description of the king and what God will accomplish through him. Thus, the king will be "righteous" (RSV) ("triumphant," NRSV), for he will keep God's covenant and rule in justice (v. 9). He will be "saved" ("victorious," NRSV) by God, for

God will bestow his favor on him and cause him to prosper (v. 9). And he will be "humble," for he will ride on a lowly donkey and not on a mighty steed of war (v. 9). Through this king, God will destroy the tools of war, bring peace to the nations, and institute his universal reign (v. 10).

In the oracle of salvation, the prophet portrays God as renewing the covenant he made with David (v. 11; 2 Sam. 7:8-16). In remembrance of this covenant, God will cause also those exiles that yet remain in captivity to return to Jerusalem.

In the New Testament, Matthew looks back on the prophet's prediction of the rise of a Davidic king and the salvation God will accomplish and regards this prediction as fulfilled. In 21:1-11, Matthew quotes Zech. 9:9 as he describes Jesus' entry into Jerusalem: Mounted on a donkey, Jesus rides into Jerusalem in humility and peace while the crowds appeal to him as the Son of David for salvation (21:1-11). To be sure, in Matthew's eyes this salvation for which the crowds shout is accomplished by God in Jesus' cross. Regardless, in the appearance of David's greater Son the hope of the prophet has found its realization.

Still, to say that the prophet's hope has been realized is not to say that it has been exhausted. On the contrary, Matthew recasts this hope so that it finds a new focus in the end-time return of Jesus and the age of salvation he will inaugurate. In this form we Christians today share in the prophet's hope.

Our hope in the ultimate triumph of God in Christ is a lively and powerful one. It explains, for example, how we can live in a world that seems so totally besieged by the forces of evil and yet not become cynical about others, pessimistic about the future, or callous toward the needs of the world. We do not become cynical about others, for we know that in Christ God proffers salvation to the whole of humankind. Nor do we become pessimistic about the future, for we know that God, through the agency of his Son, governs history and will, at the end, purge his creation of evil. Nor do we become callous toward the needs of the world, whether those of people or of the environment. The world, redeemed by God in Christ, is being guided by God toward its final redemption at the end of time. In knowledge of our own redemption and in anticipation of this final redemption, we act even now as agents of redemption.

SECOND LESSON: ROMANS 7:15-25a

To preach a sermon on Rom. 7:15-25 is at once a privilege and a challenge. It is a privilege because of the text's theological profundity. It is a challenge because commentators have long puzzled over how to interpret it.

Who is the "I" of whom Paul speaks in 7:15-25? St. Augustine and Martin Luther understood it to be Paul's own reference to himself as a Christian. The Christian, as Luther explained, is at once saint and sinner. In 7:15-25, Paul explores the depths of his inmost self and vividly describes the struggle that the Christian experiences in trying to lead a life of obedience to God.

As tempting as it is to take the text this way, Paul's earlier remarks make this impossible. Here in Romans 7, Paul describes sin as an enslaving power. In Romans 6, however, Paul states categorically that the Christian is one who has died to sin and is no longer its slave (6:2, 6-7).

On the assumption that the "I" of 7:15-25 does indeed constitute a reference by Paul to himself, it makes better sense to understand Paul as using it to refer to himself in the time prior to his conversion to Christ. What we have in 7:15-25, therefore, is Paul the Christian reflecting on his earlier life as a Pharisee. And because Paul regards the Jew and especially the Pharisee as the epitome of the religious person, we can go so far as to say that Paul employs the pronoun "I" in 7:15-25 as a reference both to himself as a Pharisee and to the religious person in general.

To capture the intention of 7:15-25, we do well to start with the law. In Paul's view, the law is holy, just, and good (7:12). The problem, however, is that sin has taken the law captive (7:7). Hence, although the law holds out to one the promise of life (7:10), the moment one endeavors to gain life by following the law, one unwittingly falls under the control of sin. The irony, therefore, is that although the law is good in itself, sin uses it as tool to lead one not to life but to death (7:10-11). Having taken the law captive, sin uses it to accomplish its evil purposes.

Accordingly, in looking back on his life as a Pharisee, Paul sees himself as having been caught in a dilemma he did not at that time perceive. On the one hand, Paul found that he desired to do what the law says is good and leads to life. On the other hand, he discovered that he continually fell short of this goal: He simply could not accomplish the good he strove to do (7:17-18). Why not? Because, Paul says in retrospect, he was enslaved to sin. As the slave of sin, he not only did not do the good he desired to do but he actually did the evil he did not want to do (7:21-23). Consequently, Paul found that he could not understand his own actions (7:15): What he desired to do he could not do, and what he hated to do, this he did. As Paul reflects in Romans on this dilemma, the latter suddenly impels him to exclaim: "Wretched man that I am! Who will rescue me from this body of death?" (7:24).

Because Paul's statements in 7:15-25 have to do with his earlier life as a Pharisee, the preacher will necessarily ask what this text has to say to people who are already "in Christ." Such, after all, are the congregants the preacher addresses.

To us who are in Christ, this text conveys a message that is at once positive and negative. In 7:25, Paul himself touches on the positive aspect of this message when he declares, "Thanks be to God through Jesus Christ our Lord!" As a result of the salvation that God has accomplished in the death and resurrection of Jesus Christ, we Christians have been removed from the sphere where sin reigns and placed in the sphere where Christ reigns. Under Christ's lordship, we are free to do God's will and to walk in newness of life. In knowledge of this freedom Paul cries out in thanksgiving to God.

Negatively, although we Christians have indeed been freed by Christ to do the will of God, we nonetheless still live in "this age" and not in the "age to come." In this age, we are yet vulnerable to the onslaughts of sin and evil. Continually, we are enticed to sever our relationship to God and to give ourselves over again to the rule of sin. By graphically depicting the kind of bondage in which sin once held even such a religious person as himself, Paul exhorts us to hold fast to Christ and to be on our guard against all of sin's wiles.

GOSPEL: MATTHEW 11:25-30

Matthew 11:25-30 is a composite of three groupings of Jesus' sayings, two of which many preachers might prefer not to deal with and one of which is a preacher's delight. At a time of misfortune or tragedy when congregants are in need of words of comfort, preachers readily turn to Jesus' solicitous words in vv. 28-30: "Come to me, all you that are weary and are carrying heavy burdens . . .". By contrast, preachers appear less eager to broach the issues Jesus raises in vv. 25-26 and v. 27. The reason is that in these two groupings of sayings, Jesus' pronouncements seem either to describe God as less than gracious or to ascribe to Jesus himself an ultimacy that prevailing opinion says no one has a right to claim in this world of many religions and differing views of God.

In vv. 25-26, Jesus asserts in effect that God deliberately conceals his revelation from the wise and understanding. But how could this be? objectors ask. Is not Jesus' assertion at odds with a far more basic notion of God, namely, that God always reaches out in grace to people, regardless of how undeserving they may be? In v. 27, Jesus declares that he alone is the one through whom God reveals himself to humans. But if God reveals himself exclusively through Jesus, objectors respond, what about all the people of the world who have never heard of Jesus? Are they to be thought of as in some sense shut off from God? Is it not more reasonable to assume that God reveals himself equally well to all religious persons throughout the world?

To grasp the intention of Jesus' sayings in vv. 25-26, it is necessary to explore the context. Previously, Matthew has depicted Jesus as carrying out a ministry of teaching, preaching, and healing, where he has proffered salvation to Israel (4:17—11:1). Now, in the section in which 11:25-30 is situated, Matthew tells of Israel's response to Jesus, which is one of repudiation (11:2—16:20). With a view to his repudiation Jesus asserts in 11:25-26 that God has hidden his revelation ("these things") from the wise and understanding. From Matthew's perspective, God is in control of history. If, therefore, Israel has repudiated Jesus, such repudiation must, in some mysterious way, have been part of God's divine plan.

Matthew takes pains to show that Jesus has in mind not present or future events, but only events that have already taken place (11:25). In other words, Matthew would make it crystal clear that Jesus is not to be construed as saying that because Israel has thus far repudiated him, God forever closes himself to Israel. On the contrary, only two verses later Jesus summons all Israel to come to him and therefore also to God (11:28).

In v. 27, Jesus does indeed lay claim to ultimacy in terms of mediating God's revelation to humans. Moreover, to Matthew's way of thinking this claim is also fundamental to the Christian faith. Still, if this claim is not to be misunderstood, one must take note of the role it plays within the theology of Matthew. Within Matthew's theology, does this claim become the basis for speculation about how God relates to people who have never heard the name of Jesus? Or does Matthew use it as a device for fostering Christian arrogance toward other religions? The answers are emphatically negative. No, one of the main purposes to which Matthew puts Jesus' claim to finality is to give grounding to the Christian mission to the nations. As Matthew conceives of it, the church's mission is not an exercise in imperialism or intolerance. Instead, it is the means whereby God graciously reaches out to proffer salvation to all people. In engaging in mission, Christians are sharing with the world the most precious gift God has bestowed on them, salvation in Jesus Christ.

In vv. 28-30, Jesus summons all Israel to come to him. Those "that are weary and carrying heavy burdens" are those who desire to lead a life of obedience to God (v. 28). In coming to Jesus, these persons will find "rest," or salvation (v. 28). Also, as they take Jesus' "yoke" upon themselves and "learn from him," they internalize Jesus' teaching and emulate him as their example (v. 29). Indeed, Jesus' yoke is "easy" and his burden is "light" (v. 30); they are so because Jesus does not leave his disciples to their own devices but remains with them and sustains them as they follow him.

In sum, the preacher who adopts 11:25-30 as the basis for his or her sermon has rich opportunity to proclaim both the oneness of Jesus with God, his gracious Father, and the oneness of Jesus with his followers. In an age that often seems to have lost its bearings, this is a powerful message congregants are eager to hear.

Eighth Sunday after Pentecost

Lutheran	Roman Catholic	Episcopal	Common Lectionary
Isa. 55:10-11	Isa. 55:10-11	Isa. 55:1-5, 10-13	Exod. 2:11-22
Rom. 8:18-25	Rom. 8:18-23	Rom. 8:9-17	Rom. 8:9-17
Matt. 13:1-9	Matt. 13:1-23	Matt. 13:1-9, 18-23	Matt. 13:1-9, 18-23

FIRST LESSON: ISAIAH 55:10-11

Chapters 40–55 of Isaiah are customarily referred to as Second—or Deutero—Isaiah, which is also the name given to the prophet who was responsible for them. By and large, these chapters are thought to have originated in Babylon before and after its fall to Cyrus, king of Persia (539 B.C.). Although preachers today can find in any of the Old Testament prophets a figure worthy of emulation, this is especially true of Deutero-Isaiah. In several ways, he stands out as a model preacher. Deutero-Isaiah stands out first of all because he identified fully with the exiles whom he addressed. This is apparent from the nature of the tradition that has come down from him: It tells interpreters little about him. It says nothing, for example, about his age, stature, looks, or personal experiences, and it treats even his call in fleeting fashion (40:6, 9). Indeed, Deutero-Isaiah recedes behind the words he utters to such an extent that the reader encounters him only as a voice. How is one to explain this phenomenon? Perhaps the best explanation is that the message Deutero-Isaiah proclaimed was meant as much for himself as it was for his fellow exiles. Like them, he too was weary and beset by doubts. Like them, he too desperately needed to hear the message of salvation God had entrusted to him. In Deutero-Isaiah, one does not have to do with a haughty preacher who addressed his hearers with a condescending mien. Just the opposite, Deutero-Isaiah took his place beside his hearers and knew himself to be admonished, renewed, or exhorted by the very message he directed at them.

Deutero-Isaiah also stands out as a model preacher because the message he delivered was timely. On the one hand, Deutero-Isaiah aligned himself with Isaiah and Jeremiah before him and repeated their message

53

of doom (e.g., 43:28). His concern in so doing was to stress that such prophecy had now been fulfilled. On the other hand, Deutero-Isaiah was quick to recognize that the situation in which the exiles found themselves was fundamentally different from before. Because they had been punished for their idolatry and disobedience, they were in need of a new word from God. As a result, Deutero-Isaiah gave pride of place in his preaching to the announcement of salvation. As one indication of this, he does not begin his book by threatening judgment but by speaking words of solace on behalf of God, "Comfort, O comfort my people, says your God" (40:1). Every word has its time and place, and it is the mark of preachers who are sensitive to their hearers that they do not become purveyors of religious jargon or commonplace banalities but preach a well-aimed word that strikes the right target at the right time.

Third, Deutero-Isaiah serves as a model for preachers in that he dared to rely on the word of God to accomplish what it said. This is where the text comes into play. It constitutes a similitude that reiterates at the close of the book what Deutero-Isaiah also affirms at the outset. In 40:6-8, Deutero-Isaiah declares that whereas people are as transient as the grass that withers, the word of God will endure forever. Here in 55:10-11, Deutero-Isaiah asserts that just as rain and snow have the certain effect of causing grain to sprout and grow, so the word of God has the certain effect of accomplishing God's purposes. God's word is sure; what God says will come about.

This is the one side of the coin. The other side is the fourth reason that Deutero-Isaiah stands out as a model preacher: He powerfully exhorts God's people to receive God's word in faith. Commentators have long called attention to the unusual way in which Deutero-Isaiah heaps up imperatives. One place he does this is in the immediate context of 55:10-11 (see vv. 1-7). Prominent among these imperatives is Deutero-Isaiah's summons to the exiles to "incline your ear" and to "listen, so that you may live" (v. 3; see also v. 2). As confident as Deutero-Isaiah was that God's word would accomplish God's purposes, he also knew from Israel's past that unless the people heard and believed God's word, it would not effect the change in them that God desired. In looking to the immediate future, Deutero-Isaiah was certain that God was about to do a new thing. This very certainty, however, also engendered in him the deep concern that God's people might mistakenly ignore and even scorn God's word and thus banish themselves from

54

the very salvation that God was about to inaugurate on their behalf. As a model preacher, therefore, Deutero-Isaiah vigorously summoned the exiles to faith in God's word. In this way, too, he struggled mightily to win the minds and hearts of the exiles for the saving word God had entrusted to him.

SECOND LESSON: ROMANS 8:18-25

In a high-tech society that thrives on living for the moment, the present is all that matters. To all intents and purposes, there is no yesterday and there is no tomorrow. The time is always right now, and right now is the time for instant joy, instant success, and instant gratification. Paul's understanding of the present could not be more different. In Rom. 8:18-25, Paul characterizes the present as a time of suffering, groaning, and hope.

In describing the present as a time of suffering (8:18), Paul is not wallowing in gloom and doom but is concerned that the Christian life imitate the life of Christ (8:17). To Paul's way of thinking, Christ's death was the key event of his life. In his death, Christ identified himself with a fallen humanity that was alienated from God and enslaved to sin. Through his death, Christ destroyed the power of sin and reconciled humanity with God. Raised from the dead by God, Christ promises all those who rely on him that they will one day share in his glorious life.

As is clear, the fundamental movement in this pattern of Christ's existence is from death to life. So it is with Christian existence. The Christian is one who has died with Christ and will live with Christ. In the meantime, the Christian suffers with Christ (8:17). What such suffering may entail varies greatly. To be sure, it may mean that one must endure the brickbats of a world that is hostile to Christ. In this connection, Paul himself points with pride to the many insults, hardships, calamities, and persecutions that he experienced (e.g., 2 Cor. 11:21b—12:10). Still, what Paul basically means when he speaks of suffering with Christ is that the Christian, under the lordship of Christ, lead the kind of life that Christ led, one that honors God and serves others. To such a life Paul sees the Christian called.

Besides being a time of suffering, the present is also a time of groaning (8:23). To groan, as Paul defines it, is to "wait with eager longing" (8:19). While all who belong to Christ long eagerly, so does the creation

(8:22). What both believers and creation long for is the renewal, or regeneration, of all things that will take place at the consummation (8:19-23).

Until recently, the notion that creation might be groaning for ultimate renewal was an aspect of Pauline theology to which interpreters paid little more than lip service. To many, this notion appeared rather farfetched. Whatever the atrocious things we humans may do to one another, the environment seemed beyond our capacity to destroy. Now, however, we are no longer so confident of creation's power to restore itself. We look aghast at the damage being inflicted upon nature as oil spills befoul coast lines, the ozone layer is depleted by chemicals, lakes and forests are rendered dead by acid rain, water and land are poisoned by toxic wastes, whole species of fish, foul, and wild life are made extinct by acts of human folly, and the planet's air is made unfit for breathing. As Paul says, the creation itself longs to "be set free from its bondage to decay" (8:21).

Precisely because of these formidable difficulties, the present is likewise a time of hope. Just as suffering gives rise to eager longing, so eager longing gives rise to hope. Those belonging to Christ hope for the "glory" that will attend the renewal of all things at the end of this age (8:18, 20-21). This glory is for both creation and those who are Christ's; their true destiny is to share in the majesty of Christ (8:17, 21).

All too frequently, one still hears the old canard that Christian hope disregards the present and amounts to little more than the expectation of pie in the sky in the great by and by. In reality, nothing could be further from the truth. Just as Christ did not turn away from the world but redeemed it, so Christians who suffer with Christ, who long eagerly for the transformation of all things, and who hope to attain to the glory of the coming age do not turn away from the world but toward it. Unlike the ancient Gnostics, who adjudged only the realm of spirit to be good and looked upon all matter, including the human body, as evil, corrupt, and deserving of destruction, Christians see themselves as Christ's ambassadors whose task and joy it is to reclaim the world for Christ. As Christ's ambassadors, Christians proclaim the gospel so that people might be freed from bondage to sin and death, brought under the lordship of Christ, and enabled to walk in newness of life. And equally, Christians work as caretakers on behalf of the environment exactly because God has not abandoned his creation to decay but is guiding it toward its ultimate renewal and glorification. In the final analysis, the power of Christian hope is that it enables Christians to persevere no matter what in their imitation of Christ to "save" the world.

GOSPEL: MATTHEW 13:1-9, 18-23

Although Matthew penned his version of the parable of the sower almost nineteen centuries ago, it is uncanny how well it speaks to the situation of many Christians today. Since Matthew himself has provided the parable (13:1-9) with an interpretation (13:18-23), the preacher perhaps does best to follow Matthew's lead and approach the parable ✓ by way of its interpretation.

The role the parable of the sower plays within Matthew's Gospel is not difficult to discern. In 4:17—11:1, Matthew recounts Jesus' ministry to Israel, whereby he proffers Israel salvation. Beginning with 11:2, Matthew describes the response of Israel—both crowds and leaders—to Jesus, which is one of rejection. Reacting himself to his rejection by Israel, Jesus in chapter 13 addresses the crowds in parables. As Matthew has Jesus observe in v. 13, the reason he addresses the crowds in parables is that they have already shown themselves to be blind, deaf, and without understanding toward him. In that he addresses them in parables, therefore, he addresses them in speech that they cannot understand and thus confirms them in their obduracy. But if the crowds ✓ do not understand Jesus' parable of the sower, who does? As Matthew indicates in vv. 18-23, the disciples understand his parable.

Literally, the parable of the sower (13:1-9) combines into one story four similitudes. With the aid of the interpretation (13:18-23), one can formulate these similitudes and understand their intention. All four have to do with hearing and understanding the word of the kingdom (vv. 19, 23). The word of the kingdom is the good news that in Jesus, God has drawn near with his rule, thus inaugurating the end-time age of salvation (4:17, 23). Or, to put it another way, the word of the kingdom is the good news by which Jesus invites people to become his disciples.

The first similitude (vv. 4, 19) is this: Just as, in the process of sowing, some seeds fall on the path and the birds come and eat them, so there are those people who, having heard the word, do not understand it and Satan comes and snatches it out of their hearts. This similitude envisages new Christians who are yet vulnerable. Some new Christians enter the church without fully understanding either what it stands for or what the ramifications of being a Christian are. Once in the church, they discover that they are not as fully committed to its faith and life as they had thought. Correlatively, they find that former ways of life that are incompatible with their new-found faith still hold strong attraction for them. The upshot is that they become confused over where their allegiance lies and regretfully solve their problem by reverting to the familiar life they had left behind.

The second similitude (vv. 5-6, 20-21) may be formulated as follows: Just as, in the process of sowing, some seeds fall on rocky ground and are withered by the sun because they have no root, so there are those people who, having heard the word, receive it with joy yet fall away as soon as they encounter trouble or persecution because of it. This similitude is self-explanatory. As long as there is no stigma attached to being a Christian, many people are pleased to be members of the church. The moment, however, it costs them to be a Christian—whether personally, socially, or professionally—they disassociate themselves from the church and its faith.

The third similitude (vv. 7, 22) runs like this: Just as, in the process of sowing, some seeds fall among the thorns and get choked by them, so there are those people who, having heard the word, become so preoccupied with the cares and riches of the world that their faith remains barren and produces no fruit. The scene sketched in this similitude is an all-too-familiar reality to most preachers. In a society in which materialism reigns supreme, Christians everywhere are hard pressed not to give first billing in their lives to the demands of the world.

Finally, the fourth similitude (vv. 8, 23) lauds those who become true Christians: Just as, in the process of sowing, some seeds fall on good soil and bear much fruit, so there are those people who, having heard the word, understand it and lead bountiful lives of Christian service. This similitude amplifies words Jesus has spoken earlier in Matthew's Gospel: "You will know them by their fruits" (7:16). Despite whatever temptations and difficulties congregants encounter, there is a strong contingent in virtually every congregation that attends eagerly to the proclamation of the gospel and attests by their deeds to their commitment to Christ. For such, the heavens praise God!

Ninth Sunday after Pentecost

Lutheran	Roman Catholic	Episcopal	Common Lectionary
Isa. 44:6-8	Wisd. of Sol. 12:13, 16-19	Wisd. of Sol. 12:13, 16-19	Exod. 3:1-12
Rom. 8:26-27	Rom. 8:26-27	Rom. 8:18-25	Rom. 8:18-25
Matt. 13:24-30	Matt. 13:24-43	Matt. 13:24-30, 36-43	Matt. 13:24-30, 36-43

FIRST LESSON: WISDOM OF SOLOMON 12:13, 16-19

The Wisdom of Solomon may be described as a long poetic work. Since it purports to convey the words of King Solomon, the "embodiment" of wisdom, its name dutifully reflects this claim. In reality, the author of Wisdom is unknown, though scholars believe that he was a Jewish intellectual residing in Alexandria and steeped in both his own religion and Hellenistic philosophy. Although the date of the book is also unknown, scholars tend to identify it with either the reign of Caesar Augustus (30 B.C. to A.D. 14) or that of the emperors immediately following him, Tiberius (A.D. 14–37) or Caligula (A.D. 37–41).

The situation in which Wisdom was written seems clear enough. Apparently, the prevailing mood in Alexandria was one of great hostility between Jews on the one hand and Greeks and Egyptians on the other. Because the Greeks and Egyptians viewed the Jews as unwelcome strangers whose religion was primitive and manners uncouth, the Jews reacted by asserting the superiority of their religion and way of life over Hellenism. To strengthen the religious and communal resolve of his fellow Jews, the author of Wisdom vigorously attacks pagan and Egyptian idolatry (chaps. 13–15), extols Dame Wisdom as the one who imparts knowledge of God and the world (6:12—9:18), and appeals in general for absolute fidelity to God's covenant with Israel.

Toward the end of his book, the author of Wisdom launches into two lengthy excursuses, the first of which deals with God's sovereign governance of the world (11:15—12:27). This first excursus, in turn, is itself divided into three parts (11:15—12:2; 12:3-11; 12:12-27), the last of which treats of God's benevolence toward all. Wisdom 12:13,

16-19 is embedded in this last part (12:12-27) and has to do primarily with God's graciousness. The main points the text makes are that God reigns supreme in the universe (v. 13), that he is righteous (v. 16a), and that he is merciful (vv. 16b, 18).

At first blush one might suspect that the author, in asserting that God reigns supreme in the universe (v. 13), is headed in the direction of defending the notion that God can do whatever he wishes because, after all, "might makes right." In reality, however, the contention of the author is just the opposite: Although God is absolutely sovereign, the astonishing thing is that he does not act like us humans, especially the ungodly (2:18), and live by the rule of might.

Theologically, this is an affirmation that bears stressing. In our society, virtually no sector of existence is not governed by the rule of might. This "might" is largely that of money or of political or institutional power and influence. Whether one thinks of dishonest politicians, greedy corporate executives, or unscrupulous officials or individuals, including also some clergy, untoward experiences have conditioned the public to believe that regardless of what such persons say about family, nation, faith, or principle, they are actually using their positions to control others and serve their own interests. God, the author of Wisdom insists, is not like this!

Instead of operating by the rule that might makes right, God, the author insists, employs his utter sovereignty to demonstrate that he is righteous (v. 16a) and merciful (vv. 16b, 18). In speaking of God's righteousness, the author has in mind God's sense of justice. As one who is just, God does not ignore iniquity but punishes it (12:12). Before acting to punish, however, God shows forbearance so that sinful people and nations might be brought to repentance (v. 19). Indeed, even when God does act to punish, he does so with a mild hand (v. 18).

These statements about God serve both to sober and to hearten us. Living as we do in an age that makes light of God's wrath and prefers to believe that his love precludes him from taking any account of sin, the affirmation that God is just and not eternally patient of sin is necessary for us to hear. Not to speak of God's wrath and to stress only his love is, finally, to cheapen his love and rob it of its meaning and power. By the same token, to speak of God as slow to punish, compassionate in judgment, and eager to bring people to repentance is to speak words of grace to all those who, in awareness of their sins, look to God for pardon and mercy.

The final word of the text concerns the way God's people are to respond to the message that he is sovereign, righteous, and merciful: Like God, they, too, are to be "kind" (v. 19). To be kind means, in effect, to imitate God, that is to say, to refuse to live by the rule that might makes right; to work for justice in the world; and, while being intolerant of sin, to rejoice in the gift of repentance by which God draws people to himself and makes them the recipients of pardon and mercy. In short, to respond to the message of the text is to be shaped by the wisdom of God.

SECOND LESSON: ROMANS 8:26-27

Except in pentecostal and charismatic circles, congregants do not often hear sermons that focus on the Holy Spirit. Although Rom. 8:26-27 has to do with the Spirit as intercessor, Romans in general and chapter 8 in particular tell us much about Paul's overall understanding of the Spirit. By making the Spirit the object of attention, the preacher has the unique opportunity to explore with the congregants what it means to confess in the third article of the Apostles' Creed, "I believe in the Holy Spirit . . .".

In Pauline parlance, talk about the Holy Spirit is talk about the power and presence of God. Moreover, the aim of such talk is eminently practical in nature: It serves to relate God's powerful presence to the daily lives of Christians.

As Paul reflects on the death of Christ, he sees the power of God manifesting itself as love: Through Christ's death, God reconciled hostile humanity to himself (5:8, 10). In raising Christ from the dead, God manifested his power as life (8:11). In the rite of baptism, this same power of God unites us with Christ so that we participate in Christ's death and receive the sure promise that we will also live with him (6:3-5, 8). Through such union with Christ, the power of God destroys sin's power to rule over us (8:6-7) and places us in the sphere where Christ rules. In this sphere, we may be said to be "in Christ" (8:10) or "in the Spirit" (8:9), and the Spirit dwells in us (8:9). All in whom the Spirit dwells are members of the "body of Christ."

Indwelt by the Spirit, we no longer live according to the "flesh" (8:4). To live according to the flesh is to have a mind-set that is hostile to God and that neither does his will nor pleases him (8:7-8). In contrast, we Christians live in close communion with God as God's children (8:14). God invites us to approach him as Father, and the Spirit leads us to cry out to him, "Abba! Father" (8:15-16; Gal. 4:6). As God's children, we become heirs of glory, that is, fellow heirs with Christ (8:17; Gal. 4:7). Also, the Spirit endows us with a mind-set whereby we produce the fruit of the Spirit, namely, "love, joy, peace, patience, kindness, generosity, faithfulness, gentleness, and self-control" (Gal. 5:22). In a word, the Spirit fosters in us right conduct.

Nor is this all. As those in whom the Spirit dwells, we also experience the Spirit as the "first fruits" (8:23) or the "first installment" (2 Cor. 1:22; 5:5) of things to come. As the first fruits, the Spirit enables us even now to anticipate the magnificent harvest with which God will grace us at the end of this age, the glorious redemption of our bodies. As the first installment, the Spirit serves as God's pledge to us that he will one day bestow on us the gift of eternal life, which is life purged of death. Consequently, the presence of God's powerful Spirit in us emboldens us to face the future with confidence.

Correlatively, the Spirit also lives within us to intercede on our behalf. This is the emphasis of Rom. 8:26-27. When Paul speaks of Christians as being "weak" and not knowing "how to pray," he shoots a well-aimed arrow directly at us. Both in our mind and in the popular mind of the culture, prayer tends to be construed as an exercise in which those praying induce God to do what they want. In the normal course of daily life, prayer becomes something of an adjunct to positive thinking and, in times of crisis, a means for securing deliverance or some special blessing. Ensnared as we are in this kind of thinking—in this weakness and ignorance—Paul stresses that the Spirit helps us. The way the Spirit helps us is by leading us to pray "as we ought"; the Spirit leads us to pray in accordance with God's will. Still, once we recognize how God would have us pray, we recognize as well that the true purpose of prayer is not to move God to do what we want but to move us to do what God wants. By bringing our will into alignment with God's will, the Spirit shows itself to be God's power not only for salvation but also for sanctification.

GOSPEL: MATTHEW 13:24-30, 36-43

Sober interpreters of the American scene warn that society is becoming dangerously fragmented as rival groups of all kinds assert their own interests to the detriment of the common good. Nor has this trend left churches and denominations unscathed. In the first century, Matthew's community was forced to wrestle with a related problem, namely, whether to separate itself from the society around it. In the parable of the tares (13:24-30) and its interpretation (13:36-43), we have a window that provides us with a good view of the debate.

Matthew shows, by pairing the parable of the tares with an interpretation, that he regards the parable as allegorical. What this suggests, in turn, is that the interpretation is the avenue by which to approach the parable.

When one reads the parable through the lens of its interpretation, its meaning jumps to light. The story begins by depicting the struggle that is taking place in this age between the risen Jesus and his archenemy, who is the devil, or evil one (13:24-25, 37, 39). This struggle is over the allegiance of humans, and the devil, as a wicked usurper, has brought many under his control (13:25-26). The result is that humans have become divided into two groups: Whereas the one group, which gives its allegiance to the risen Jesus, comprises the children of the kingdom, the other group, which gives its allegiance to the devil, comprises the children of the evil one (13:38). As these two groups intermingle, the children of the kingdom find themselves in a quandary: Is it not imperative that they separate themselves from the children of the evil one? While some insist that this is in fact what they must do (13:28), the risen Jesus himself will not hear of it (13:29a). During this age, he avers, the children of the kingdom are not to separate themselves from the children of the evil one. The reason, he says in an interesting comment, is that if they force such separation, they run ✓ the risk of inadvertently doing harm to some of their own (13:29).

From this allegorical parable one learns much about both the theology and situation of Matthew. Theologically, Matthew understands God— or the risen Jesus—and evil to be the controlling powers of the universe. Fundamentally, therefore, people give their allegiance to either the one or the other, and the one to whom they give their allegiance is determinative of their character and destiny.

To modern society's way of thinking, such notions as these, which are commonplace in the world of the New Testament, are obsolete. Today, society trades not in "black and white" but in intermediate shades. One reason for this is that society has effectively done away with evil and sharply limits how much influence God can be expected to have on humans. The upshot is that people are regarded as being morally directed by neither God nor evil but simply by themselves and others. Once this view of morality asserts itself, distinctions tend to get blurred: Nothing is deemed to be godly or evil, and everything is regarded as some vague blend of the two. In contrast to this type of thinking, Matthew reminds us that we humans are not morally free agents who take our direction simply from ourselves. On the contrary, we all stand under the aegis of another, whether it be God or, fatefully, the evil one.

Through the vehicle of this parable, one also catches a glimpse of the situation of Matthew. Matthew's community was at home in a hostile society and subject to persecution (5:10-12; 10:17-19; 24:9). With an eye to the preservation of the community, some within it apparently counseled that the community should separate itself from the world (13:28). Invoking the authority of the risen Jesus, Matthew warned against following such counsel: For the community to separate itself from the world would be for the community to cut itself off from those in the world who would otherwise become children of the kingdom (13:29).

As the church today confronts forces in society that increasingly seem inimical to it, one does not have to listen hard to hear voices urging it to adopt a more defensive posture vis-à-vis society. To some, the negative influence of society seems so pervasive and overwhelming that they believe that if the church is not to compromise its faith and life, it must be much more concerned to shield itself from society and to see after its purity. Indeed, the best way the church can influence society is by becoming a conventicle that calls attention to itself precisely by remaining apart from society. To those who take this position, the parable of the tares and its interpretation counsel just the opposite course of action. The risen Jesus has entrusted the church with a mission in the world, to gather to itself all those destined to become children of the kingdom. To carry out this mission, the church dare not turn its back on the world but, holding fast in allegiance to the risen Jesus, proclaim its message in the world. After all, the task the church has been given is not to save itself but the world.